ISO 45001 Implementation

ISO 45001 Implementation

How to Become an Occupational Health
and Safety Champion

Mehrdad Soltanifar

Routledge
Taylor & Francis Group

A PRODUCTIVITY PRESS BOOK

First published 2022
by Routledge
605 Third Avenue, New York, NY 10158

and by Routledge
2 Park Square, Milton Park, Abingdon, Oxon, OX14 4RN

Routledge is an imprint of the Taylor & Francis Group, an informa business

© 2022 Mehrdad Soltanifar

Library of Congress Cataloging-in-Publication Data
A catalog record for this book has been requested

ISBN: 978-1-032-21055-1 (hbk)
ISBN: 978-1-032-21054-4 (pbk)
ISBN: 978-1-003-26653-2 (ebk)

DOI: 10.4324/9781003266532

Typeset in Garamond
by Apex CoVantage, LLC

Contents

Preface

The importance of occupational health and safety cannot be underestimated. Minimising work-related injury and illness is a major challenge for countries, managers, unions, and especially workers. Organisations should ensure that their workers' health and safety are not at risk as a result of the work they do. Having a planned approach to managing occupational health and safety helps businesses to effectively protect their workers from work-related illnesses, injuries or even death.

Much has been written on the topic of occupational health and safety and on the adoption of ISO 45001 standards in workplaces, but most of these writings appear to primarily target professionals who have a prior knowledge of the concepts and requirements of this ISO standard. This book is aimed at any individual or organisation that wants to implement an effective occupational health and safety management system. No assumptions have been made about my readers' prior knowledge. This book's audience may be not only experienced professionals but also people with no prior experience or knowledge of the structure and definitions of ISO 45001 or of health and safety management.

This book presents guidance for understanding all the requirements of the standard, illustrated using practical examples and techniques from industries. While clarifying each requirement of the standard, it also discusses the steps needed to achieve the requirement, areas that auditors may check, and mandatory or voluntary documents that may be maintained or retained to demonstrate conformity with the requirement.

This book is divided into ten chapters. Chapter 1 enables the reader to understand the importance of establishing an occupational health and safety management system to protect workers and provide a healthy and safe working environment. It also introduces the new structure of ISO standards, called Annex SL, which aims to assist organisations to implement a number of management system standards simultaneously.

The history of ISO 45000 and the family of occupational health and safety standards are discussed in Chapter 2. Moreover, benefits of implementing an occupational health and safety management system based on ISO 45001:2018 requirements have been illustrated in this chapter. This chapter also provides a brief introduction to each clause of the standard along with the ISO 45001 certification process.

Chapter 3 explains the terms and definitions used in the ISO 45001:2018 standard, which is necessary for understanding its concepts and requirements.

The remaining chapters define the requirements of the ISO 45001:2018 from determining the context of the organisation to performance evaluation and continual improvement. Each chapter gives a comprehensive diagnosis of the clauses of the standard, a step-by-step guide to implement the requirements, potential questions asked by auditors during the certification audit, and a list of mandatory and voluntary evidence for each clause.

Acknowledgements

I wish to thank all the people who introduced me to the world of occupational health and safety and continuous improvement, and who have supported, taught, and provided valuable information during the undertaking of writing this book and in my professional career. The list of names is too extensive to include here, but I am indebted, in particular, to Ken Heap, Andrew Wills and Christel Fouche, who peer-reviewed my work and helped form my views on various aspects of ISO 45001. They each brought different perspectives and interpretations to my consideration of this subject.

Finally, I would like to thank my dear family for their warm support throughout the years. Both my parents were teachers and I wish to honour them by continuing the gift of teaching.

About the Author

Mehrdad Soltanifar, PhD, is a senior consultant, trainer, business development manager, and researcher working on occupational health and safety, quality, and environmental management systems. Starting his career in 2010, he has extensive experience in improving organisations' processes. In conjunction with significant growth and expansion of multi-million-dollar companies, Mehrdad has assisted several organisations in various industries by reviewing health and safety, quality, and environmental aspects of their businesses to ensure that the foundations are solid and capable of catering for the anticipated growth ahead.

In addition to working with businesses in New Zealand and Australia to produce their own integrated management systems to meet the requirements of ISO 45001, ISO 9001, and ISO 14001, he has held various managerial posts at Manco Engineering Group—a company specialising in ground-breaking technologies in the waste recycling industries and custom-built rail electrification construction for major infrastructure projects around the world. Mehrdad gained his PhD degree in engineering from Auckland University of Technology. Currently living in Auckland, New Zealand, he is interested in process development and in continuously improving and transferring his knowledge and experiences to others.

Chapter 1

Introduction

Over 2 million people worldwide die every year due to work-related accidents and illnesses, which correlates to over 6,000 deaths every day (International Labour Organisation, 2020). Globally, there are around 340 million occupational accidents and 160 million victims of work-related injuries and illness each year (International Labour Organisation, 2020). Occupational health and safety (OHS) is a major challenge for many organisations.

Regardless of the size and nature of their business, organisations should protect their people and provide a safe and healthy working environment. They should identify the potential health and safety risks present in their workplace and take appropriate action to keep their workers free from harm. Occupational safety focuses on potential safety hazards that can cause injury. Occupational health, on the other hand, looks at potential health issues such as occupational medicine, occupational hygiene, and primary health care, including the well-being of workers.

Organisations need to manage multiple aspects of their operations that require them to comply with different sets of standards such as quality, health and safety, and environment. As the ISO standards become more widely accepted, well-established organisations tend to simultaneously implement a number of management-system standards such as ISO 9001, ISO 14001, and OHSAS 18001.

Considering this, ISO decided to develop their standards using a structure called Annex SL (renamed Annex L in the 2019 edition), which consists of ten category clauses to assist with the integration of these management systems. New versions of ISO 9001 and ISO 14001, which follow the new

DOI: 10.4324/9781003266532-1

structure, were published in 2015. However, OHSAS 18001 has been superseded by ISO 45001, published in 2018. ISO 45001 is an internationally accepted framework to manage health and safety in the workplace, conforming to ISO's Annex L, and it follows the same high-level structure as other international standards.

For organisations that want to implement an OHS management system (OHSMS) based on the ISO 45001:2018 standard but are not familiar with its structure and definitions, it often takes a significant amount of resources to understand the requirements of the standard and plan their implementation. This book provides guidance in establishing an OHSMS linked to the requirements of ISO 45001:2018. It aims to explain all the requirements of ISO 45001:2018 clause by clause to provide guidance to:

■ Organisations preparing for ISO 45001:2018 implementation
■ Individuals who want to build a career in OHS
■ Health and safety practitioners and managers who want to improve their OHS performance
■ OHS consultants who prepare their clients for ISO 45001:2018 certification audits
■ Internal and external auditors who audit OHSMS

In addition to the requirements of the standard, this book includes industry best practices, methods, and techniques to address these requirements. While clarifying each requirement of the standard, it also discusses the steps needed to achieve the requirement, areas that auditors may check, and mandatory or voluntary documents that may be maintained or retained to demonstrate conformity with the requirement.

However, the reader should bear in mind that approaches to address ISO 45001 are not limited to the ones explained in this book. OHS is a wide-ranging subject with much research regularly being published. Interested parties should therefore investigate and research other methodologies to find the most suitable approaches for their organisation.

Chapter 2

Understanding the Basics

2.1 What Is ISO 45001?

The International Organisation for Standardization (ISO) in an international standards setting body. Founded in 1947 as an independent, non-governmental organisation, ISO is the largest standards organisation with more than 160 members. Each member belongs to the national body that represents standardisation in their country. Through its members, ISO brings together experts to share knowledge and develop standards to provide solutions to industrial and commercial challenges (ISO, 2021).

ISO 45001, introduced in March 2018, is part of the ISO 45000 family of standards. ISO 45000 standards guide organisations towards improving workers' health and safety in the workplace. Similar to other ISO family standards, ISO 45000 has one auditable standard, which is ISO 45001. ISO 45001 is an internationally recognised standard that sets the requirements for creating, implementing, maintaining, and improving OHSMS. The OHSMS is a proactive framework that assists organisations to protect people from occupational injuries and ill health. It is intended to be used by organisations, irrespective of their size and industry.

ISO has categorised management system standards into 'type A' and 'type B.' Type A standards contain requirements against which an organisation can claim conformance, whereas type B standards do not specify requirements but usually offer definitions, clarifications, and guidance on how the

DOI: 10.4324/9781003266532-2

requirements can be fulfilled. ISO 45001 is the only type A standard in the ISO 45000 family. Type B standards published to date include:

- ISO 45002:2018—General guidelines for the implementation of ISO 45001:2018
- ISO 45003:2021—Guidelines for managing psychological risks at work
- ISO 45005:2020—Guidelines for safe working during the COVID-19 pandemic

Organisations can only get certification for their management system against type A standards. Therefore, to be audited by a certification body (CB) for their OHSMS, organisations must follow the requirements of ISO 45001. However, they may use other standards in this family as a guide for their OHSMS implementation.

The following outcomes were considered by the ISO members when developing ISO 45001:2018:

- To enable organisations to provide a healthy and safe working environment by identifying and managing their risks and improving their OHS performance
- To be applicable and relevant to all types and sizes of organisations and industries, and to accommodate diverse geographical, cultural, and social conditions
- To specify the requirements of an effective OHSMS
- To enable organisations to demonstrate conformity with the requirements
- To be able to integrate with other management systems including Quality Management System ISO 9001 and Environmental Management System ISO 14001, among others

The intended outcomes of the OHSMS are to prevent work-related injury and ill health and to provide safe and healthy workplaces through the elimination of hazards and the minimisation of OHS risks. It provides the mechanisms to assist organisations to make their workplaces safer and healthier. Implementation of an OHSMS based on the ISO 45001 requirements can also assist organisations to better engage with their workers, create a culture of continual improvement, and improve the organisation's credibility.

Moreover, there are other benefits involved in obtaining ISO 45001 certification. Many organisations invest in ISO certifications to become more competitive in their market and attract new customers and clients. Both private and public tenders often include criteria related to health and safety. Implementing a health and safety management system and being accredited by a third-party CB may be the difference between winning a tender or losing it to a competitor.

Organisations can also avoid financial losses caused by fines or delays due to incidents by implementing an effective OHSMS. "If you think safety is expensive, try an accident," is a popular quote attributed to Stelios Haji-Ioannou, the EasyJet entrepreneur. Furthermore, ISO 45001-certified organisations often attract lower insurance premiums as they can demonstrate a strong commitment to protecting their workers.

ISO 45001 is based on the 'plan-do-check-act' (PDCA) methodology (see Figure 2.1) and provides a process-oriented approach for documenting and reviewing the structure, responsibilities, and documented information required to achieve effective health and safety management in an organisation. PDCA is the concept of a continual cycle, with the prime objective being to drive forward improvements.

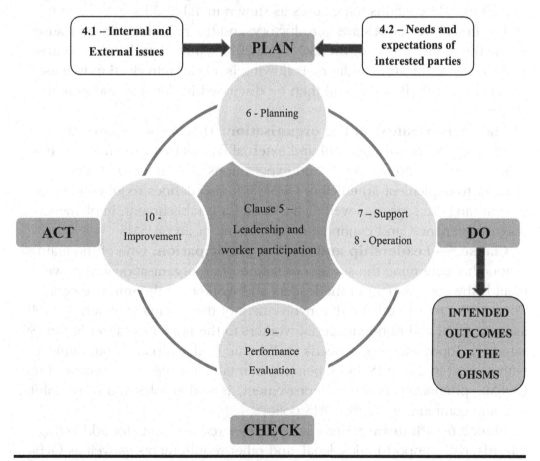

Figure 2.1   PDCA concept on ISO 45001:2018.

Table 2.1 ISO 45001:2018 Clauses

Clause 1	Scope
Clause 2	Normative references
Clause 3	Terms and definitions
Clause 4	Context of the organisation
Clause 5	Leadership and worker participation
Clause 6	Planning
Clause 7	Support
Clause 8	Operation
Clause 9	Performance evaluation
Clause 10	Improvement

ISO 45001:2018 contains ten clauses as shown in Table 2.1.

The first three clauses are introductory, and the remaining seven clauses define the requirements of the ISO 45001:2018 standard and will be evaluated by the certification auditors. Following is a brief introduction to these seven clauses. Each clause will then be discussed in detail in subsequent chapters.

Clause 4—Context of the organisation: This clause requires an organisation to identify internal and external factors that can affect its strategic objectives, and the needs and expectations of its interested parties, in order to implement an efficient OHSMS. It also defines requirements for determining the scope, as well as the need for establishment, implementation, maintenance, and continual improvement, of an OHSMS.

Clause 5—Leadership and worker participation: One of the main factors that determine the success or failure of an organisational improvement is the commitment of the leaders and workers to the improvement. This section tries to ensure the involvement of the top management as well as managerial and non-managerial workers to the implementation of the ISO standard. Top management needs to illustrate leadership and commitment with respect to the OHSMS by being accountable for the effectiveness of the OHSMS, promoting continual improvement, assigning roles and responsibilities, and communicating the OHS policy.

Clause 6—Planning: This clause defines requirements for addressing hazards, risks, opportunities, legal, and other requirements as well as OHS objectives and the planning needed to achieve them.

Clause 7—Support: To ensure that OHSMS is aligned with other activities of the business, organisations should verify that they have the right resources to achieve their intended outcome. These resources may include elements such as competent people, adequately documented information, and appropriate means of communication.

Clause 8—Operation: This clause is focused on establishing operational controls to eliminate the OHS hazards, the management of changes, and emergency preparedness and response.

Clause 9—Performance evaluation: Requirements in this clause underscore the importance of considering what, how, and when to measure the performance of the OHSMS and determine the elements that influence the effectiveness of the system. Once the processes are in place, organisations should determine mechanisms to monitor and measure the OHSMS performance with the involvement of top management.

Clause 10—Improvement: This clause describes the requirements needed to improve the company's OHSMS over time by identifying issues and nonconformances, taking corrective actions to rectify these issues, and examining and eliminating the root causes of the nonconformances to avoid recurrence of the issues. Continual improvement is the sweetest outcome of any management system. It is a type of mindset that indicates, no matter how well you think your organisation performs, there are always areas for improvement.

2.2 Process for Gaining ISO 45001 Certification

To be ISO 45001 certified, organisations need to implement OHSMS conformance within the requirements of ISO 45001. Once the OHSMS is in place, organisations can contact a CB to conduct certification audits. The CB will assign a certification auditor (or team of auditors) to verify the organisation's conformance against the ISO 45001:2018 requirements through certification audits. ISO 45001 certification verifies that the organisation has established and implemented an effective OHSMS, increasing stakeholder confidence and giving the organisation a competitive advantage.

ISO 45001 certification audits are completed in two stages. The first stage is the 'readiness review' audit where the auditors determine if the organisation has established an OHSMS and is ready for the second-stage audit. During the first stage, the auditors will review the organisation's documented information and site-specific conditions. The auditors will also review the scope of the management system and gather information on processes, procedures, regulatory requirements, and the levels of control the organisation has established.

The stage 1 audit usually takes one to two days depending on the size and complexity of the organisation. Once the stage 1 audit is completed, the auditors will provide an audit conclusion report advising whether the organisation is ready to move to the next stage and outlining areas of concern that could be considered to be nonconforming, for the stage 2 audit.

Usually, several months after the stage 1 audit (depending on the nature of the areas of concern and availability of the auditors and auditees) the auditors will return to audit the entire management system and confirm that all the requirements of the standard have been met. It would be optimal if there is at least a three-month history of OHS implementation for auditors to see during this stage. The stage 2 audit report highlights any nonconformance identified by the auditors. Certification cannot be issued until corrective actions have been taken by the organisation and have been verified by the auditors.

These certification audits can be conducted on-site or remotely (also referred to as 'virtual' audits). In an on-site audit, the auditors will visit the organisation's sites and conduct the audit in-person. The number of audit days depends on factors such as the size and complexity of the organisation. This is the most common way of auditing. However, since 2020, due to the COVID-19 pandemic, remote audits have increased significantly.

Regardless of the audit type, the audit process is the same and is based on the ISO 19011 standard. ISO 19011 provides a guideline for auditing management systems, including guidance on managing audit programmes, the principles of auditing, and the evaluation of competence of individuals involved in the audit process (ISO 19011:2018). As defined in ISO 19011, a standard audit programme should contain the four phases described in Figure 2.2.

Since the main purpose of this book is to assist auditees, here we discuss the processes of the third phase where the auditees are involved. An audit session starts with an opening meeting where the auditors and the management team will first meet. The lead auditor manages this meeting to confirm the audit plan with the auditees, introduce the audit team, and ensure that all audit activities can be performed. This meeting usually takes around 30 minutes. It is important that the top management attends either the opening meeting or the closing meeting (ideally both) to show commitment to the organisational improvement.

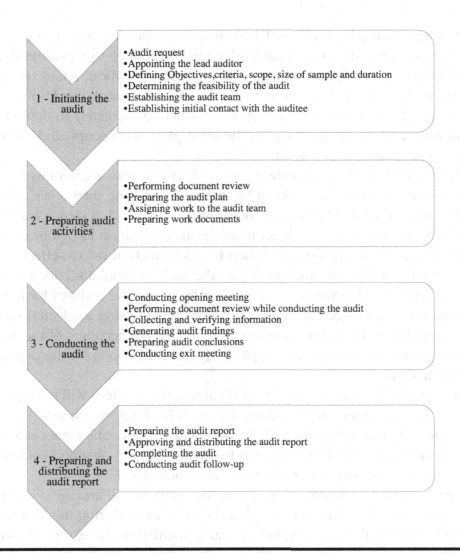

Figure 2.2   Four-step audit programme (ISO 19011:2018).

After the opening meeting, the auditors will conduct a documented information review, interviews, and observation of the work environment to ensure that the organisation has the systems in place to satisfy all the requirements of the ISO 45001:2018 standard. Competent auditors, based on their previous experience and the nature of the auditee's business, may focus on specific parts of the OHSMS. Some auditors may spend more time on risk assessments; others may focus on employee competency and training. However, the whole management system must be audited.

During the audit, the audit team members will communicate regularly to exchange information, determine the progress of the audit, and reassign work among themselves (ISO 19011:2018). Communication may also be necessary between the audit team leader and the auditee to report on the audit's progress, significant findings, and any concerns about issues outside the scope of the audit. If the audit evidence suggests that the audit objectives cannot be met, the auditee will be informed immediately to determine appropriate action such as changing the audit plan, audit scope and objectives, or termination of the audit.

During the audit session, auditors will collect evidence relevant to the audit objectives, scope, and criteria by methods including interviews, observations, and a documented information review. Obtained evidence leading to audit findings should be subject to adequate verification to demonstrate that requirements are being met. When it is not practical or cost-effective to examine all available information during the audit session, auditors will use audit sampling. Audit sampling is a process by which the auditors form a conclusion about a large data set (population) by assessing a selected subset of the population. However, sampling may reduce the accuracy of the audit conclusions as the determined samples may not fully represent the population's characteristics.

Once objective evidence has been obtained, the auditors will evaluate it against the audit criteria to determine the audit findings, which may indicate conformity or nonconformity with the audit criteria. Identified nonconformities will be reviewed with the auditee to ensure that the obtained evidence is accurate and that the nonconformities are understood.

After gathering adequate information, the auditors will arrange a closing meeting to present the audit findings and conclusions. During this meeting, the lead auditor will briefly explain the audit highlights, the extent of conformity with the audit criteria, achievement of audit objectives, scope, and fulfilment of audit criteria.

The auditors will describe positive aspects of the auditee's health and safety management system as well as opportunities for improvements (OFIs). If there are any identified nonconformities, the auditors will explain the process that needs to be followed. However, if there are no major nonconformances, the auditors will advise the organisation that they will recommend to the CB that the organisation conforms to the requirements of the ISO 45001:2018 standard.

Chapter 3

Terms and Definitions

Before we discuss the requirements of the standard, some important terms need to be defined in order to understand the OHSMS [Source: ISO 45001:2018, ISO 19011:2018]:

Audit: Systematic, independent, and documented process for obtaining evidence and evaluating it objectively to determine the extent to which the audit criteria are fulfilled

Audit findings: Results of the evaluation of the collected audit evidence against audit criteria

Competence: Ability to apply skills, knowledge, and experience to successfully achieve intended results

Conformity: Fulfilment of a requirement

Consultation: Seeking views and opinions before making a decision

Continual improvement: Ongoing effort to enhance performance

Corrective action: Action to eliminate the cause(s) of nonconformity or an incident and to prevent a recurrence

Documented information: Information required to be controlled and maintained by the organisation, and the medium in which it is contained

Hazard: Potential source of injury and/or ill health

Incident: Occurrence arising out of a work-related activity that could or does result in injury and/or ill health

Injury and ill health: Adverse effect on the physical, mental, or cognitive condition of workers, which the organisation should try to avoid

DOI: 10.4324/9781003266532-3

Interested party: Person or organisation that can affect, be affected, or perceive itself to be affected by the decisions and activities of the organisation

Management system: A set of interrelated policies, procedures, and responsibilities organised into a structured system of processes to help the organisation to realise and achieve its goals and objectives

Nonconformity: Non-fulfilment of a requirement

Objective: Result to be achieved

Objective evidence: Data supporting the existence or verity of something

Occupational health and safety management system (OHSMS): A management system for achieving OHS policy and objectives

Opportunity: Circumstance or set of circumstances that can lead to improvement

Outsource: Arrangements with an external organisation to perform part of the organisation's process

Participation: Involvement in decision-making processes such as attending OHS committee meetings and management review meetings (MRMs)

Policy: A formal document expressed by the top management defining the intentions and direction of the organisation

Procedure: Specified way to carry out a process

Process: Set of interrelated activities which transform inputs to outputs

Requirement: Needs and expectations (obligatory or generally implied) that are required to be met

Risk: Effect of uncertainty that, if it occurs, has a positive or negative impact

Risk assessment: The overall process of estimating the magnitude of risk and deciding whether the risk is tolerable

Top management: A person or group of persons responsible for directing the organisation at the highest level within the scope of the OHSMS

Worker: Person performing tasks under the control of the organisation. It includes managerial and non-managerial workers, workers of external providers, contractors, and agency workers

Chapter 4

Context of the Organisation

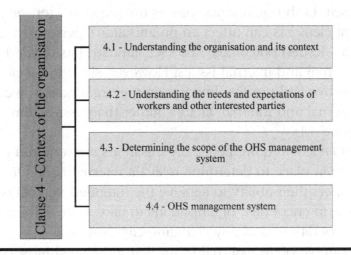

Overview of Clause 4—Context of the organisation (ISO 45001:2018).

The intended benefits of the OHSMS might not be achieved in full if the organisation does not adequately determine relevant factors affecting its health and safety performance. Thus, the requirements of ISO 45001 start with the identification of the strategic direction of the organisation and various internal and external elements that might inhibit or exacerbate the achievement of its health and safety objectives.

4.1   Understanding the Organisation and Its Context

The first step for implementing any management system is to understand the environment in which the organisation operates. An organisation is not an

DOI: 10.4324/9781003266532-4

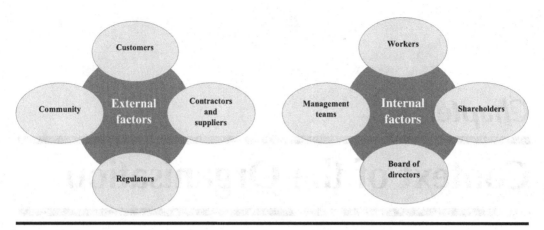

Figure 4.1   Internal and external factors (ISO 45001:2018).

island unto itself. Each organisation has its unique characteristics and conditions. Different elements can affect an organisation's performance in terms of achieving its desired outcomes. The ISO standard has divided these elements into external and internal issues. However, since these elements can have both negative and positive impacts on the organisation, we will refer to them as external and internal 'factors' rather than 'issues' throughout this book (See Figure 4.1).

To meet ISO 45001 requirements, organisations are required to have an ongoing system in place to determine relevant internal and external factors that can affect their ability to achieve the intended outcomes of their OHSMS. This is to encourage organisations to take a proactive approach to address these conditions and any changing circumstances.

A recent example of an external factor that influenced most of the world's organisations is that of the additional risks brought about by the COVID-19 situation, which led to extra control measures being required at workplaces, such as physical distancing, and problems such as a shortage of masks and sanitisers. Other examples of external factors include:

■ Cultural, social, and political factors that have positive or negative impacts on health and safety in the workplace
■ Legal factors that can affect an organisation's compliance with legal health and safety requirements
■ Environmental factors such as noise and dust from neighbouring organisations
■ Contractors, competitors, or suppliers that could impact an organisation's OHS

■ New knowledge of products and their effect on health and safety in the workplace

Examples of internal factors that may impact an organisation's health and safety performance are having a new CEO or making changes to the top management's commitment to the OHSMS. Other examples of internal factors include:

■ Changes in roles and responsibilities of management or personnel that can affect OHSMS
■ Changes in an organisation's health and safety policies and objectives
■ Capabilities in terms of resources, knowledge, and competence
■ Changes in the needs and expectations of workers in relation to their health and safety at work
■ Introduction of new products, materials, services, tools, software, premises, and equipment
■ Working time arrangements
■ Working conditions

Management should regularly review internal and external factors that may affect the success of their OHSMS. The output of this activity provides input into the consideration of risks and opportunities.

4.2 Needs and Expectations of Interested Parties

Each organisation has a unique set of interested parties whose needs and expectations change and develop over time. Thus, organisations should have an ongoing system in place to determine interested parties that are affected by the organisation's activities and to understand their health and safety needs and expectations. This will assist organisations to consider what health and safety requirements they need to fulfil to meet the needs of the parties being affected by the organisation's activities.

The first and most obvious interested party of an organisation is its workers. To meet the needs and expectations of workers, companies should provide safe and healthy working conditions and processes, eliminate potential hazards and reduce risks, and address other health and safety–related matters that concern their workers.

However, the interested parties of an organisation are not limited to its workers. Legal and regulatory bodies have a responsibility to ensure the enforcement of OHS regulations. Suppliers provide products that may have serious OHS implications for workers or users. Organisations can also affect their local community by improving community health and minimising risks of the organisation's negative impact on the public. Therefore, various other interested parties may be identified by an organisation.

A critical part of identifying the needs and expectations of interested parties is to determine which of these are a legal requirement and are mandatory due to being incorporated into laws and regulations. The organisation may also decide to voluntarily meet other needs and expectations of interested parties, such as being certified to ISO 45001, which is not a legal requirement. The needs and expectations of interested parties may change over time. Therefore, organisations should monitor and review information about these interested parties and their relevant requirements on an ongoing basis and apply necessary changes to the OHSMS as required. Outputs from this information will be addressed when planning and establishing the OHSMS.

4.3   Determining the Scope of the OHSMS

Once the organisation has identified factors that can affect its OHSMS, it should then define the boundaries and applicability of the OHSMS. Defining the 'scope' is a vital step because after that the concept of the 'organisation' in the OHSMS is limited to what has been defined in the scope.

The OHSMS scope can include the organisation as a whole or a specific site or function of the organisation. The OHSMS scope should include everything under the influence and control of the organisation that can affect its health and safety performance. Organisations cannot exclude activities, products, and services that have an impact on their OHS performance or have the potential to become a legal obligation.

Organisations should maintain the scope of their OHSMS as documented information and make it available to their interested parties. The OHSMS scope should define physical locations of the organisation and processes, products, services, and activities under the organisation's control that have a potential impact on its OHS performance.

4.4   OHS Management System

The last section of clause 4 of the standard requires organisations to establish, implement, maintain, and continually improve the organisation's

OHSMS by reviewing it regularly. This is the most comprehensive sub-clause of the standard as it covers all the other clauses and requires organisations to conform with all requirements of ISO 45001. Organisations should decide how they want to fulfil the requirements of the standard, including the level of detail and extent to which they:

■ Establish processes to have confidence that they are controlled, carried out as planned, and achieve the intended outcomes of the OHSMS.
■ Integrate requirements of the OHSMS into its various business processes (e.g. procurement, human resources, sales, and marketing).

Steps to Complete

1. Management meetings need to be conducted to identify external and internal factors that affect the organisation's OHS performance and determine plans to manage these factors. Attendees of this meeting can be top management, the OHS manager, managerial and non-managerial workers, and workers' representatives. Results of these meetings may be recorded (not mandatory) through meeting minutes, revised objectives, corporate policies, and business planning documents. Agenda items to be considered in these meetings need to:

   a. Identify external/internal factors (can be done through SWOT and PESTEL analysis)
   b. Discuss how each factor affects the organisation
   c. Identify the risks relevant to this factor
   d. Establish plans to mitigate the risks
   e. Appoint a responsible person/department for each factor
   f. Decide on the frequency of reviewing external/internal factors

2. Management meetings need to be conducted to identify interested parties, their needs and expectations and determine which of these needs and expectations could become legal and other requirements. Attendees of this meeting can be top management, the OHS manager, managerial and non-managerial workers, and workers' representatives. Results of these meetings may be recorded (not mandatory) through meeting minutes, revised objectives, corporate policies, and business planning documents. Agenda items to be considered in these meetings should:

   a. Identify interested parties
   b. Assess their needs and expectations

    c. Determine if needs and expectations can become a compliance obligation

    d. Assess the impact of non-compliance on the organisation

    e. Determine risks and opportunities relevant to the needs and expectations

    f. Appoint a responsible person/department for the needs and expectations

    g. Decide on the frequency of reviewing interested parties and their needs and expectations.

3. Management meetings need to be conducted to determine the boundaries and applicability of the OHSMS to establish its scope. Attendees of this meeting may be top management, OHS manager, managerial and non-managerial workers, and workers' representatives. Results of these meetings should be recorded (mandatory) according to the OHSMS scope. Agenda items to be considered in these meetings should:

    a. Identify the scope of the organisation's OHSMS

    b. Identify any exclusions

    c. Provide justification for exclusions

Auditors Will Check That

- External and internal issues have been determined.
- External and internal issues have been identified, and how they have been identified.
- The organisation has determined its interested parties and their needs and expectations.
- Needs and expectations of interested parties that can become a legal obligation have been identified.
- The scope of the OHSMS has been determined.
- Any exclusions have been properly justified.
- The scope of the OHSMS has been maintained as documented information.

Records

- Scope of the OHSMS (mandatory)
- List of external and internal factors (non-mandatory)
- List of interested parties and their needs and expectations (non-mandatory)

Chapter 5

Leadership and Worker Participation

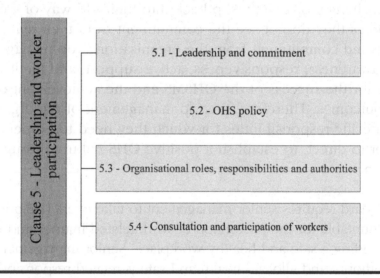

Overview of Clause 5—Leadership and worker participation (ISO 45001:2018).

Without the proper support from top management and workers, any management system is doomed to failure. Top management of the organisation and its workers should understand what is trying to be achieved, why it is being implemented, and what benefits it can bring to the organisation. Thus, ISO 45001 is highly focused on the involvement and commitment of the leaders and workers, which is not limited to this clause but prevails throughout the whole standard.

DOI: 10.4324/9781003266532-5

This clause of the standard requires that both senior management and workers demonstrate a clear commitment to OHS management. Senior management should take the overall responsibility and be accountable for protecting workers and integrating health and safety management into the organisation's daily business processes. Moreover, this clause also emphasises the consultation and participation of workers in different aspects of the OHSMS, such as taking part in hazards and risks' identification and the development of OHS policies and objectives.

5.1   Leadership and Commitment

One of the biggest challenges of implementing any management system in an organisation is the resistance to change from its people. Workers (both managerial and non-managerial) often push back against the change, or quietly slip back into their old way of working as soon as they do not see the commitment from their managers. Leadership and commitment from the organisation's top management, including awareness, responsiveness, active support, and feedback, are critical for the success of the OHSMS and the achievement of its intended outcomes. Therefore, the top management of the organisation assumes specific responsibilities for which they need to be personally involved or to direct, to establish a positive OHS culture throughout the organisation.

A) The standard requires senior management to take overall responsibility and be accountable for the prevention of work-related injuries and ill health, and for providing a safe and healthy workplace. Senior management can delegate authority and allocate health and safety–related responsibilities to other workers, but the final responsibility remains with the senior management. Workers need to understand and recognise that their health and safety are important to the top management and efforts are being made to improve their working conditions.

Steps to Complete

1. Ensure that commitment of the top management is evident from top management's roles and responsibilities.
2. Ensure that the top management is aware that they should accept the overall accountability for the prevention of work-related injuries and ill health.

3. Train top management, if necessary, to understand their responsibilities with respect to health and safety in the workplace.
4. Include OHS matters on the agenda of senior management and board meetings and maintain minutes to demonstrate that it is entrenched in the organisation's business processes.

Auditors Will

■ Interview the top management and review their job descriptions to check if they are aware of their responsibilities to ensure the health and safety of their workers and other workers who are being influenced or directed by the organisation.
■ Check if OHS matters are discussed in the top management-level meetings.

Records

■ Senior management job description (mandatory)
■ Minutes of senior management and board meetings (non-mandatory)

B) Senior management should ensure that OHS policies and objectives are established and are in line with the strategic direction of the organisation. Establishing effective policies and objectives allows senior management to contextualise health and safety in the organisation's activities. Effective OHS objectives should be specific, measurable, achievable, relevant, and time-bound (SMART).

Steps to Complete

1. OHS policy to be reviewed and preferably signed and dated by the top management.
2. OHS objectives to be determined with the participation of the top management, managerial and non-managerial workers, and workers' representatives.
3. OHS objectives to be in line with the organisation's strategic business plans (mission, vision, and core values).

Auditors Will Check That

■ Top management has been involved in establishing OHS policy and objectives.
■ They are compatible with the organisation's short-term and long-term strategies.

Records

■ Approved OHS policy (mandatory as per clause 5.2)
■ Approved OHS objectives (mandatory as per clause 6.2), including:

  * objective
  * objective start date
  * objective completion date
  * responsible person
  * monitoring methodology
  * monitoring frequency

C) Top management should ensure that the OHSMS has been integrated into the organisation's business processes. This is a challenging yet important step towards implementing the OHSMS. In many organisations, health and safety is a separate process being managed by only a few individuals, and when they leave the company the process will often stop. If companies fail to integrate their health and safety systems into their daily processes, most probably their OHSMS will also eventually fail, as it can be seen as gratuitous and unnecessary by their workers. Senior management should ensure that OHS procedures such as risk and hazard identification, internal audits, management reviews and workers' consultation and participation are integrated with other processes of the organisation.

Steps to Complete

1. Conduct meetings with the participation of top management, managerial and non-managerial workers, and workers' representatives to determine how OHSMS processes can be integrated with other business processes, and maintain meeting minutes. Examples of integration may include:

    a. Risk and hazard identification, which can be done along with other regular workplace inspections, OHS committee meetings, toolbox meetings
    b. OHS audits, which can be conducted along with other regular inspections, quality, and environmental audits
    c. OHS management reviews, which can be included on the agenda of regular business meetings
    d. Consultation with and participation of workers, which can be considered while developing OHS policies, objectives, annual training sessions, incident investigations, etc.

Auditors Will Check

■ What efforts have been made to integrate OHSMS into daily business processes?

Records

■ Evidence of integration of OHSMS with other business processes (non-mandatory)

D) Senior management should ensure that adequate resources have been provided to implement, maintain, and improve the OHSMS. To satisfy the requirements of this clause, senior management should have a proper understanding of what resources are required and what resources are available. Resources required can include competent personnel, adequate OHS-related tools and equipment, sufficient finances, and other resources to comply with the standards and regulatory requirements.

Steps to Complete

1. Identify resources required in management meetings, OHS committee meetings and toolbox meetings, and maintain minutes of the meetings as evidence.
2. Assign competent people by top management to the OHSMS tasks. If competent workers are not available, employ or provide training.
3. Allocate an adequate budget for the OHSMS implementation.

Auditors Will

■ Interview management and workers, and check records such as management meeting minutes to determine if top management has been involved in reviewing the adequacy of resources (human, intellectual, and financial resources) to implement, maintain, and improve the organisation's OHSMS.

Records

■ Evidence of identification of required resources, allocation of competent personnel to OHS-related tasks, evaluation, and allocation of adequate budget to OHS matters (non-mandatory).

E) Top management should communicate the importance of implementing an effective OHSMS and conforming to the ISO 45001 requirements. It is the responsibility of the senior management to ensure that the procedures and practices related to the OHSMS are communicated efficiently throughout the organisation to all workers and other interested parties. Examples of these communications include management meetings, safety committee meetings, toolbox talks, trainings, OHS briefings, and posters.

Steps to Complete

1. Conduct meetings with key health and safety workers, including the top management, to decide what communication is necessary, how it should be carried out, and who is responsible for doing it.
2. Communicate to interested parties (by top management) the reasons for implementing OHSMS and the benefits it can bring to the organisation.

Auditors Will Check

■ What has been communicated and how
■ Which tasks, practices, and changes trigger communication within the organisation
■ That the means of communication is aligned with the purpose

Records: Evidence of communicating the importance and benefits of implementing the OHSMS (non-mandatory)

F) Top management should ensure that the OHSMS achieves its objectives. After determining the OHS objectives in clause 5.1.b, senior management should ensure that achievement plans are defined. Senior management is also responsible for regularly reviewing the progress of the defined plans.

Steps to Complete

1. Conduct meetings with top management to determine the following, and maintain meeting minutes, including:

   a. OHS objective
   b. Objective start date
   c. Objective target date
   d. Responsible person/department to achieve the objective
   e. Monitoring methodology
   f. Monitoring frequency
   g. Responsible person(s) to monitor the progress of the objective.

2. Communicate objectives to relevant interested parties and assign tasks to the responsible person/department.
3. Review the progress of the objectives in MRMs, OHS committee meetings, and toolbox talks.

Auditors Will Check That

- OHS objectives are defined and measurable.
- Objective achievement plans are defined.
- Objective processes are reviewed regularly by the top management.
- OHS performance reports are sent directly to senior management by the OHS manager.

Records

- Objective achievement plan (mandatory as per clause 6.2), including:

  * objective status
  * tasks
  * responsible person or department
  * resources required
  * target date

- Objective tracking (non-mandatory), including:

  * tracking date
  * progress and completion percentage

G) Senior management should direct and support workers (both managerial and non-managerial) to contribute to the implementation, maintenance, and improvement of the OHSMS. This section covers the following sub-clauses:

- 5.1.i Support other relevant management roles to demonstrate leadership
- 5.1.k Protect workers from reprisals when reporting incidents, hazards, risks, and opportunities
- 5.1.l Support establishment of a process for consultation and participation of workers
- 5.1.m Support establishment of the OHS committees

A management system can be successful only if all the members work together and contribute to the system. Senior management should eliminate any obstacles and lead others to understand the importance of OHS.

Senior management should direct other managers by providing them with resources and training, checking their needs in regard to the OHSMS, and regularly evaluating their performance. Senior management should facilitate workers and other managers to communicate their OHS-related needs efficiently.

Moreover, there may be times where workers want to express their concerns about a potential risk or hazard or report a nonconformity they have seen in the workplace to their supervisors. In these situations, senior management should take the required steps to encourage workers to speak up and protect them from reprisal or retaliation. Senior management should take a proactive approach so that workers feel that their efforts in identifying and reporting OHS risks and hazards are valued and encouraged. It is important to ensure that workers understand how they can inform their supervisors about any potential risk and hazard and that they are protected from reprisal. This can be communicated through induction programmes, OHS briefings, toolbox talks, and so on.

Top management should also ensure that procedures and policies are established to enable workers to participate in and be consulted on OHS aspects such as risk and hazard identification, required training, finding nonconformances, and taking corrective actions. This two-way consultation can be done through toolbox talks, daily briefings, training, and OHS committee meetings. Thus, senior management should support and promote opportunities and channels for consultation with workers and ensure the effectiveness of these processes.

Steps to Complete

1. Top management to regularly review the necessary competence of other managers in their OHS-related tasks (including the ability to identify hazards and risks) and provide training if necessary. This can be done through an annual competence evaluation process.
2. Top management to regularly consult with other managers regarding the resources they need for their OHS-related tasks. This matter can be discussed in MRMs.
3. Top management to determine a process for two-way communication with workers to provide necessary OHS-related information to workers and workers' representatives and receive their concerns and feedback. Established processes should ensure that workers are being encouraged to express their concerns and they will be protected from reprisal.

Auditors Will Check That

- Competency of other managers is being evaluated, and training and other resources are being provided to them when necessary.
- Top management is involved in establishing an effective process for consultation and participation of workers.
- Workers have been interviewed to ensure that they are aware of the ways to communicate their OHS concerns and that they feel they are being protected against reprisal and retaliation.

Records

- Competence evaluation of managers reviewed by the top management (non-mandatory)
- Meeting minutes of top management with other managers in regard to identification and allocation of resources they require for their OHS-related tasks (non-mandatory)
- Procedures for consultation and participation of workers (non-mandatory)
- Information about how to communicate concerns and feedback to supervisors in workers' induction programmes (non-mandatory)

H) Senior management should promote continual improvement. Successful organisations in terms of health and safety are the ones that constantly have their eyes on potential OHS improvement opportunities and better performance. Continual improvement is a mindset of always looking for areas that can be improved. Companies should build continual improvement into their health and safety culture, and this starts with the senior management. Senior management's commitment demonstrates to workers what behaviours and actions will be rewarded or punished, which influences their attitudes in terms of health and safety in the workplace.

This aspect can also include sub-clause 5.1.j, which is about the responsibility of the senior management in developing, leading, and promoting the health and safety culture in the organisation. Top management's involvement and commitment can make a significant contribution to changing workers' attitudes and behaviours in relation to health and safety in the workplace. Senior management performing OHS requirements, participating in OHS activities, allocating adequate resources to the OHSMS, and promoting it is considered as an act of motivation to others.

Steps to Complete

■ Top management to determine processes to promote continual improvement of OHSMS by receiving suggestions, performance evaluation, training, rewarding, and brainstorming meetings to identify areas for improvement, then taking the required steps to implement these processes

Auditors Will Check That

■ Recommendations for improvement opportunities are being discussed in OHS-related meetings.
■ Senior management encourages employees to follow OHS at work and promotes the achievement of OHS objectives.
■ Adequate resources have been allocated for continual improvement.

Records

■ Evidence of top management reviewing recommendations for OHS improvements and taking action accordingly (non-mandatory)
■ Evidence of training on continual improvement for top management, managerial and non-managerial workers (non-mandatory)
■ Budgets and other resources allocated to continual improvement (non-mandatory)

5.2   OHS Policy

The OHS policy is a set of principles, stated as commitments, in which top management outlines the long-term direction of the organisation in supporting and continually improving its health and safety performance. The OHS policy provides an overall sense of direction, as well as a framework for the organisation to set its objectives and take steps to achieve the intended outcomes of the OHSMS. It is also a helpful tool to get everyone within the organisation to work towards the same goal of a safe and healthy workplace.

The standard considers senior management to be responsible for establishing, implementing, maintaining, and communicating an effective OHS policy. The OHS policy should be available as documented information; thus, it should be approved, maintained, and periodically reviewed. It should be communicated within the organisation and should be available to other interested parties either by posting it on the company's website or by providing it upon request, to ensure that all interested parties are aware of the organisation's OHS vision and direction. As the nature of risks and hazards are different in each company, the OHS policy should be relevant to the size and nature of the organisation.

The OHS policy should include the following:

■ A commitment to:

  * provide safe and healthy working conditions for prevention of work-related injury and ill health
  * fulfil all relevant health and safety legislation, regulations, codes of practice, and other requirements associated with the organisation's operation
  * eliminate OHS hazards and reduce risks
  * continually improve OHSMS
  * continually improve OHS performance
  * encourage workers to participate in decision-making processes within the OHSMS and promote OHS awareness

■ A brief description of OHS objectives or provision of a basis for setting the OHS objectives

A sample health and safety policy statement can be found in Appendix A.

Steps to Complete

1. Establishment of an OHS policy relevant to the context of the organisation to ensure all the requirements of clause 5.2 have been included.
2. Review and approval of the OHS policy by top management.
3. Distribution of the latest version of the OHS policy among interested parties (workers, contractors, customers, visitors, etc.).

Auditors Will Check That

■ The OHS policy has been determined, documented, and regularly reviewed by the top management.
■ The OHS policy is available to interested parties.
■ The OHS policy is relevant to the context of the organisation.
■ The OHS policy covers all the requirements of clause 5.2 of the standard.

Records: The OHS policy (mandatory)

5.3 Organisational Roles and Responsibilities

Individuals involved in the organisation's OHSMS should have a clear understanding of their roles and responsibilities for achieving the intended outcomes of the OHSMS. A 'role' is one's position within the organisation and 'responsibilities' are the tasks, duties, and authorities of a role. Senior management should ensure that the roles and responsibilities for the OHS-related tasks are assigned and communicated to all levels within the organisation and maintained as documented information. Delegating responsibilities to workers gives them a sense of ownership and increases their efficiency.

The more clearly the top management outlines the roles and responsibilities, the better the workers can achieve the organisation's OHS objectives. Roles and responsibilities should be designated to competent personnel and be within the control of the assigned individuals.

One of the effective tools that can be used by senior management when defining roles, responsibilities, and authorities is the 'responsibility assignment matrix' also known as the RACI (Responsible, Accountable, Consulted, and Informed) matrix. The RACI matrix defines the following:

▪ The person who is responsible for the execution of the work
▪ The person who is accountable for approving the task, whether by signing it off, delegating responsibility, or approving it once the task is completed
▪ The person who should be consulted before the work can be done
▪ The person who should be kept informed and up-to-date on the progress of the task

A sample RACI matrix can be found in Appendix B.

Assigned roles and responsibilities should be maintained as documented information, meaning that they need to be approved, documented, and regularly reviewed for effectiveness. Although the responsibilities can be delegated to others within the organisation, the ultimate responsibility for managing OHSMS resides with the top management. By assigning appropriate roles, responsibilities, and authorities to workers, senior management should ensure that:

▪ The OHSMS is implemented and maintained effectively.
▪ Processes are executed effectively, and they deliver the intended OHS outcomes.

- The OHSMS performance and improvement opportunities are reported to top management.
- Safe and healthy working conditions for the prevention of work-related injuries and ill health are promoted.
- Change management of the OHSMS is effective.

Top management is also responsible for designating an individual to perform specific tasks relevant to the OHSMS, such as ensuring that the established OHSMS conforms to the requirement of ISO 45001, and that person must report the performance of the OHSMS to the top management. Although the standard did not suggest any specific designation for this role, it is common for organisations to assign these tasks to health and safety managers or OHS management representatives.

Steps to Complete

1. Determine job descriptions relevant to the OHSMS (e.g. roles and responsibilities of senior management, health and safety manager, OHS officers, OHS auditors, head of departments, supervisors, and workers).
2. Senior management to review, approve, and distribute roles and responsibilities.
3. Senior management to ensure that the channels for receiving reports on the OHSMS performance are defined.

Auditors Will Check That

- Roles and responsibilities required for effective implementation of OHSMS have been approved and communicated by the top management.
- Workers have been interviewed to assess if they consider their assigned responsibilities are appropriate and within their control.
- Top management has set up appropriate channels to receive reports on the OHSMS performance.

Records: Approved OHS roles and responsibilities (mandatory).

5.4 Consultation and Participation of Workers

Consultation with, and participation of, workers is a key factor of success for an OHSMS. Organisations should make it clear that health and safety in the workplace is the responsibility of all employees. The standard requires an organisation to establish, implement, and maintain a process for workers' consultation and participation in all aspects of health and safety at work. Workers include all personnel performing work-related activities under the control of the organisation, including managerial and non-managerial staff, trainees, volunteers, contractors, and contractors' workers.

'Consultation' refers to a two-way communication so that workers are actively involved in the OHS-related decision-making processes and the implementation of activities undertaken within the OHSMS. 'Participation' refers to the engagement with workers, workers' representatives, and health and safety committees before making decisions on OHS performance and changes.

This requirement provides an opportunity for workers to contribute to decision-making processes that affect their health and safety at work. Workers at all levels should be encouraged to report hazards and risks and define preventive measures to be put in place. To meet the requirements of this clause, organisations should:

■ Provide mechanisms (such as worker representation), time, training, and resources necessary for consultation and participation of workers
■ Provide timely access to clear, understandable, and relevant information about the OHSMS through classroom training, reference manuals, health and safety posters, etc.
■ Identify and remove obstacles or barriers to participation (such as failure to respond to workers' inputs or suggestions, language or literacy barriers, reprisals or threats of reprisals, and policies or practices that discourage or penalise worker participation) and minimise those that cannot be removed
■ Emphasise the consultation of non-managerial workers on the following aspects:

  * determining the needs and expectations of interested parties
  * establishing the OHS policy
  * assigning organisational roles, responsibilities, and authorities, as applicable
  * determining how to fulfil legal requirements and other requirements
  * establishing OHS objectives and planning to achieve them
  * determining applicable controls for outsourcing, procurement, and contractors

* determining what needs to be monitored, measured, and evaluated
* planning, establishing, implementing, and maintaining audit programmes
* ensuring continual improvement

■ Emphasise the participation of non-managerial workers in the following aspects:

* determining the mechanisms for their consultation and participation
* identifying hazards and assessing risks and opportunities
* determining actions to eliminate hazards and reduce OHS risks
* determining competence requirements, training needs, training, and evaluating training
* determining what needs to be communicated and how this will be done
* determining control measures and their effective implementation and use
* investigating incidents and nonconformities and determining corrective actions

Organisations should consider situations where workers might feel uncomfortable raising a particular OHS issue with their supervisors or managers. This can be done through health and safety representatives (HSRs) who consult and assist workers in health and safety matters. Workers who are HSRs are deemed to represent workers in particular work groups and, as such, will undertake regular, meaningful consultation with the workers in their workgroup. Their duties include responding to OHS issues raised with them by a worker or group of workers. HSRs are then empowered to raise OHS issues formally at meetings with their supervisor or manager and may in certain circumstances contact the relevant government authority for assistance and information.

To enable the maintenance of a safe and healthy work environment, organisations should determine an issue resolution process in the event of a dispute about OHS matters. This process should provide guidelines to resolve any OHS issues in an efficient, timely, and suitable manner. Organisations may seek assistance from regulatory bodies if an OHS issue cannot be resolved satisfactorily. In attempting to resolve OHS issues, organisations should consider:

■ The degree and immediacy of the risk to workers or other people affected by the issue

■ The number and location of workers and other people affected by the issue

■ The corrective measures (temporary and permanent) that must be implemented to resolve the issue, using appropriate mechanisms to eliminate and control risks

■ The appointment of a responsible person to implement the resolution measures

■ That consultation takes place between all parties involved and affected by the OHS issue

(Appendix C illustrates an example OHS issue resolution flowchart.)

Organisations should foster a culture of open communication and discussions related to OHS and, furthermore, ensure that workers' interests are efficiently represented through formalised consultative arrangements. However, while emphasising that the consultation and participation of non-managerial workers are intended to apply to persons carrying out the work activities, it is not intended to exclude managers who are impacted by work activities or other factors in the organisation.

Steps to Complete

1. Determine a procedure for consultation and participation of workers. It can include the following:

   a. How to provide necessary information to the workers and how to receive their concerns and feedback on OHS-related matters
   b. How workers elect their OHS representatives (e.g. show of hands, secret ballot)
   c. How the OHS committee functions
   d. How workers can be involved in OHS decisions such as required training, incident investigations, identification of hazards and risks, identification of OFIs
   e. How to resolve OHS issues arising in the workplace
   f. Who is responsible to ensure the effective implementation of this procedure

2. Ensure top management reviews this procedure, approves, and distributes it to relevant personnel.
3. Inform new workers about this procedure in their induction programme.

Auditors Will Check That

- A process for a two-way consultation and participation with workers in regard to development, planning, implementation, performance evaluation, and actions for OHSMS improvement has been defined.
- Workers are involved in defining training requirements for OHS performance.
- Workers have access to easily understandable and relevant information about OHSMS.
- Workers are involved in identifying and reducing hazards and risks.
- Non-managerial workers are involved in establishing OHS policy, objectives, and planning to achieve them.
- Non-managerial workers are involved in defining applicable controls for outsourcing, procurement, and contractors.
- Non-managerial workers are consulted on planning, implementing, and maintaining audit programmes.

Records

- Workers' participation and consultation procedure (non-mandatory), including:

  * appropriate method for participation and consultation of workers
  * functioning of the OHS committee

    - definition of OHS committee's roles
    - process for selecting workers reps
    - timetable for committee meetings
    - opportunity for agenda to be reviewed

- Minutes of OHS committee meeting (non-mandatory)
- Issue resolution procedure (non-mandatory)

Chapter 6

Planning

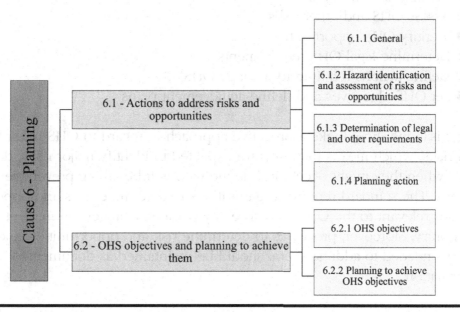

Overview of Clause 6—Planning (ISO 45001:2018).

6.1 Actions to Address Risks and Opportunities

6.1.1 General

Once the organisation has determined its context and secured management's involvement in the process, it can then plan for the implementation of an OHSMS. This phase can assist the organisation in setting up an effective management system and ensuring its continual improvement. This critical

DOI: 10.4324/9781003266532-6

step requires a comprehensive understanding of operations to establish strategic objectives and principles for the OHSMS. In a health and safety management system, unlike other business processes, there is usually no second chance. Failure in OHS planning can result in a negative impact on people's health and safety, which is why this clause is crucial in implementing an effective OHSMS.

Planning is an ongoing process of reviewing, addressing, and responding to changes in the OHSMS. While planning for the OHSMS, organisations should take into account their context, the needs and expectations of all interested parties, and the scope of the OHSMS. The standard requires organisations to take the following actions in the planning phase:

■ Identify OHS hazards
■ Assess OHS and other risks
■ Identify OHS opportunities
■ Determine legal OHS requirements
■ Define actions required to manage OHSMS
■ Set OHS objectives and define achievement plans

Organisations should take a proactive approach in regard to OHS hazards and risks, which means that they are expected to identify major risks, determine when they might occur, and define who will be taking preventive actions. The standard requires organisations to determine risks and opportunities relevant to the OHSMS before any planned changes, permanent or temporary. Moreover, processes to determine risk and opportunities, and actions needed to address them, should be maintained as documented information.

6.1.2   *Hazard Identification and Assessment of Risks and Opportunities*

6.1.2.1   *Hazard Identification*

A hazard is a source with the potential to cause harm or hazardous situations, or circumstances with the potential for exposure leading to injury and ill health. Hazard identification is a process of identifying procedures or activities that have the ability to harm workers. Hazards are detectable through various sources such as inspections, audits, reporting, committee meetings, and toolbox talks.

ISO 45001 requires organisations to establish, implement, and maintain a proactive and ongoing process for hazard identification. Workers play a vital role in identifying hazards as they are aware of the potential causes of harm and injuries. Hazard identification should be undertaken at all levels within the organisation.

It is beneficial for the hazard identification team to include both managerial and non-managerial roles, with multi-disciplinary expertise, to identify potential hazards in different kinds of circumstances and work processes. The standard requires organisations to consider the following factors when carrying out hazard identification:

■ Social factors (including workload, work hours, victimisation, harassment, and bullying)
■ Activities performed every day as part of the organisation's processes, and activities performed for special situations such as installing a new machine or testing a gantry
■ Leadership and culture of the organisation
■ Hazards arising from infrastructure, equipment, materials, substances, and physical conditions of the workplace
■ Product and service design, research, development, testing, production, assembly, construction, service delivery, maintenance, and disposal
■ Human factors
■ The way work is being performed
■ Previous incidents and audits
■ Health and safety–related documents such as equipment operating manuals and material safety data sheets
■ Potential emergency situations
■ Workers, contractors, and others who have access to the workplace
■ People who can be affected by the activities of the organisation
■ Workers at a location not under the direct control of the organisation
■ Design of work areas, processes, installations, equipment, operating procedures
■ Situations occurring in the vicinity of the workplace caused by work-related activities of the organisation
■ Situations occurring in the vicinity of the workplace caused by activities not controlled by the organisation
■ Actual or potential changes in the organisation, operations, products, activities, and the OHSMS
■ Actual or potential changes in hazard knowledge and information

The hazard identification process needs to take into account all possible sources of hazards. The common sources of health and safety hazards are:

Biological

They are substances produced by an organism that may pose a threat to human health, such as blood, medical waste, fungi, sewage, animals, bacteria, viruses, and other humans. They exist in most workplaces that involve working around other people in unsanitary conditions, labs, or the environment. When assessing a workplace for biological hazards, organisations may check whether:

- Employees work in proximity to animals, insects, or other people who may have a contagious sickness.
- The workplace is tidy and clear of fungi.
- Employees work in proximity to biological materials such as sewage.
- Employees work in proximity to sharp materials that impose biological hazards (e.g. syringes and needles) and need to be disposed of securely.

Biomechanical

They are hazards linked to manual tasks (lifting, carrying, putting down objects) that can result in musculoskeletal (bone, muscle, tendon, ligament, cartilage, and other connective tissues) damages. Workers are at risk from biomechanical hazards when a load is too heavy, too large, or difficult to grasp, or if they are required to bend and twist when handling heavy loads, or the task is repetitive. When assessing a workplace for biomechanical hazards, organisations should check if the following actions have been implemented:

- Often-used items are in easy access between knee and shoulder height.
- Heavy items are stored at waist height.
- Repetitive activities are minimised.
- Step ladders/stools are used to access items on high shelving.
- Regular rest breaks are taken.

Chemical

This hazard type includes any chemical that can cause a physical or health hazard. Chemical hazards and toxic substances pose a wide range of health hazards (such as irritation, sensitisation, and carcinogenicity) and physical hazards (such as flammability, corrosion, and explosibility). Examples of some common hazardous substances include fuels, paints, solvents, and cleaning products. Workers can be exposed by inhaling, swallowing, or through the skin, which can cause death, cancer, or damage to internal organs. When assessing a workplace for chemical hazards, organisations should check the following:

■ Procedures for storage, handling, or use of hazardous substances are clearly defined.
■ Chemical containers are labelled clearly and appropriately.
■ Gas cylinders are secured properly.
■ Chemical inventory and material safety data sheets are available.
■ Chemicals are disposed of properly.

Electrical

Electrical hazards can cause death or serious injury by electric shock (electricity passing through the body), arc flash (sudden release of electricity), or explosion caused by unsuitable electrical apparatus. Typical sources of electrical hazards are underground and overground powerlines, plugs, cables, and fixed and portable electrical tools. When assessing the workplace for electrical hazards, organisations should check the following:

■ Electrical tools have a current test and tag.
■ Extension leads are used only for temporary power supply.
■ Leads are kept clear of walkways.
■ Tags are displayed on faulty equipment.
■ Extension cords are secured to the wall or floor using tape (not nails or staples, as they can cause a fire or shock).
■ Circuit breakers and fuses are working and clearly labelled.

Hydraulic

Hydraulic system components run at significant pressures and temperatures. Hydraulics pose hazards associated with heat and stored hydraulic energy, as well as crush hazards such as falling loads when hydraulic systems fail. Hydraulic equipment can pose serious hazards such as injection injury (a jet of hydraulic fluid pierces the skin and enters the bloodstream) and burns (a hose burst resulting in the release of hot hydraulic fluid). The most common point of failure in a hydraulic system is at the fittings, where corrosion and stress-related damage are most likely to occur. When assessing a workplace for hydraulic hazards, organisations should check the following:

- Rated load is clearly marked on the hydraulic equipment.
- Circuit is hosed correctly, and protection equipment is in place.
- Hydraulic equipment is checked for pinholes in the hydraulic line.
- Galvanised fittings have not been used in hydraulic circuits.

Vehicles and Mobile Plant

These types of hazards are the ones caused by any moving vehicle in the workplace, such as forklift trucks, mobile cranes, and dollies. Moving vehicles are one of the major causes of fatal accidents in the workplace. The most common causes of injury are moving vehicles hitting or running over people, people falling off workplace vehicles, workplace vehicles overturning, and objects falling off workplace vehicles. When assessing a workplace for moving vehicle hazards, organisations should check the following:

- Workers have enough time to complete their work without rushing.
- Workers wear hi-vis clothing where needed.
- There are suitable crossing places on vehicle routes.
- Visibility is good, lights are adequate and working, and markings and signs are clear.
- Workplaces are kept tidy, potholes are filled, spills are cleaned up quickly to avoid slips and trips, and the potential to destabilise loads and vehicles is minimised.
- Shelves are fastened to the ground in locations where forklifts are in operation.
- Vehicles' fitting lights, reversing lights, horns, and other warning devices, such as rotating beacons or reversing alarms, are working properly.

Mechanical

These are the hazards that can be caused by equipment such as machines, transmissions, flywheels, couplings, sprockets, and chains. Mechanical equipment can injure people by crushing, cutting, shearing, puncturing, abrading, burning, tearing, and stretching. Injury can also occur if loose hair or clothing gets caught in equipment or a moving part. When assessing a workplace for mechanical hazards, organisations should check the following:

- Machinery is securely fenced and has an emergency stop button.
- Crushing points of the machinery are clearly marked.
- Accessible parts of the machine have no sharp edges, sharp corners, rough surfaces, or protruding parts.

Noise and Vibration

Noise is unwanted sound that can cause impairment or damage to health. Vibration refers to the "oscillatory motions of solid bodies [and] . . . arises from mechanical sources with which humans have physical contact" (McPhee et al., 2009). Noise-induced hearing loss is a well-recognised impact of noise hazard. The health impacts of vibration hazards include digestive problems and variations in blood pressure which can lead to heart problems, fatigue, and motion sickness. Although the impacts of noise and vibration hazards are different, the controls are similar. When assessing a workplace for noise and vibration hazards, organisations should check the following:

- Noise and vibration sources have been identified, eliminated, or minimised where possible.
- Hearing protection is available where hazardous noise levels exist in the workplace.
- Noisy materials such as metal components have been replaced by quieter materials such as plastic where possible.
- Machinery and equipment have been replaced with quieter types.
- Workplace noise level is being monitored regularly.
- Seats and headrests are insulated in cases where vibration can be transmitted through the seat or headrest.
- The speed of tools and equipment is limited to minimise the noise and vibration.
- The time spent by workers on noisy equipment and vibrating surfaces is limited.

Working at Height

Working at height means working in a place where a person could be injured if they fell from one level to another. It can include falling off roofs, ladders, walls, tanks, and storage racks. Falling from heights can cause fatality, serious head injury, spinal injuries, fractures, sprains, and strains. When assessing a workplace for working at height hazards, organisations should check the following:

- The right type of ladders have been selected.
- Surfaces are stable, even, and clean.
- Appropriate signage is in place.
- Harnesses are correctly used.
- Handrails have been installed where required.

Radiation

Medical facilities, nuclear sites, laboratories, and industrial radiography areas are typical locations of radiation hazards. Radiation can cause dermatitis, burns, cell damage, cataracts, changes in blood, fever, loss of hair, and death. When assessing a workplace for radiation hazards, organisations should check the following:

■ Appropriate radiation warning signs are posted at the entrances.
■ Emergency procedures and phone numbers are clearly posted.
■ Radioactive material and devices are secured to prevent unauthorised access.
■ Appropriate personnel are supplied with a radiation dosimeter.

Thermal

The exposure of workers to extreme heat or cold can result in serious illnesses and injuries, and even death. Exposure to extreme heat can occur when working with cookers, ovens, welding operations, boilers, and heaters. Cold exposure can occur in cold storage areas associated with the freezing of food products, meat-processing plants, low-temperature exterior climates, and extreme environments such as polar regions. When assessing a workplace for thermal hazards, organisations should check the following:

■ If air circulation is sufficient to allow evaporation of sweat
■ If fans are needed to keep workers cool
■ If work is carried out in direct sunlight
■ If there are heat-producing processes or equipment in the workplace
■ If work is scheduled to avoid the hottest part of the day
■ In case of cold climate, where possible, if work is undertaken in the warmest part of the day
■ If workers have access to cool/hot potable drinking water

Psychosocial

Psychosocial hazards include stress, fatigue, bullying, violence, aggression, harassment, and burnout, which can be harmful to the health of workers and compromise their well-being. Both short- and long-term exposure to psychosocial hazards at work can have a negative impact on the mental health and safety of workers. Exposure to psychosocial hazards has been linked to long-term physical and mental health issues. When assessing a workplace for psychosocial hazards, organisations should check the following:

- Any department, unit, role, or position showing higher levels of sick leave compared to others
- Trends or common themes in complaints or workplace grievances
- Industrial relations records or disputes that link to job stress or dissatisfaction in the workplace
- Understaffed work areas
- People showing signs of stress (e.g. verbal abuse, openly criticising others or the organisation, general frustration with the work environment, incivility)
- Any related and unresolved issues in minutes of meetings (e.g. workload or change in work roles)
- Evidence of a lack of knowledge and compliance with the organisation's policies and procedures related to psychological health (e.g. harassment, bullying, or discrimination)

Fire

Fire hazards can arise in a variety of environments or while undertaking certain activities. The risk of fire is more likely in situations where flammable chemicals or combustible materials are being used, but even in offices and other lower-risk environments, the risk of fire is always present. The main causes of fire in the workplace are electricity, waste material, smoking, cooking, heating appliances, and combustible materials. Organisations should identify fire hazards, develop and maintain efficient fire safety procedures, maintain appropriate fire safety equipment, and train workers about fire safety. When assessing a workplace for fire hazards, organisations should also check for the following:

- Fire alarms are tested and maintained on a regular basis.
- Suitable firefighting equipment is provided throughout the workplace.
- Regular checks are undertaken to ensure that fire safety equipment is not missing or damaged.
- Fire safety equipment is accessible and within the required distance from high-risk activities.
- Flammable solids, liquids, and gases are isolated from sources of ignition such as open flames, heated surfaces, or unprotected electrical wiring.

- Fuel storage facilities are in a clearly marked location, well separated from areas where personnel are working.
- Exit doors can be readily opened from the inside during working hours.
- 'Fire action' notices are clearly displayed throughout the workplace.
- Safe assembly point(s) for employees, outside the building, are identified.
- Smoking is prohibited in all but designated areas.

Remote and Isolated Work

Remote and isolated work refers to working activities undertaken during or outside normal working hours at a location away from an office environment where few people are involved and communication and travel are difficult. The number of people working in isolation, or remotely away from their office at a site, home, or in a vehicle, is increasing. The hazards involved in remote and isolated work occur because the worker is away from the assistance of other persons. Examples of remote and isolated work include:

- Working alone at night in a laboratory
- Working at home or outside normal working hours
- Working separately from others in another location
- Travelling long distances as part of work, such as freight transport drivers
- Working on weekends or public holidays

Organisations should ensure that a safe and healthy system of work is in place to manage hazards associated with remote and isolated work. When assessing the hazards of remote and isolated work, organisations should check:

- That the remote or isolated work is necessary
- That workers who are working remotely or in isolation are identified
- That the duration of tasks, location, proximity to medical treatment facilities and emergency responders have been considered for remote and isolated work
- That suitable controls are determined on a case-by-case basis for remote and isolated work (e.g. a list of tasks that are considered too risky for working in isolation)
- That adequate forms of communication are available and emergency communication systems are working properly

- That support systems including alarms, first aid kits, and other emergency procedures are in place
- Whether the remote or isolated worker has any pre-existing medical conditions that may increase the risk of potential hazards
- That adequate training and information are provided to remote and isolated workers

When assessing work-related hazards, organisations should review available health and safety information from authoritative sources including safety alerts, industry codes of practice, national and international standards, technical reports prepared by experts, and safety data sheets. It is very important to recognise that hazard identification is an ongoing process. Not all possible hazards can be spotted in the initial hazard identification. It is also possible that new equipment, processes, and changes introduce new hazards. Thus, different locations and workplaces should be regularly inspected for new hazards.

Steps to Complete

1. Determine a process for hazard identification. It can include techniques and methodologies to identify hazards by considering:

   a. routine and non-routine activities
   b. human factors
   c. new or changed hazards
   d. potential emergency situations
   e. affected people
   f. changes to knowledge and information
   g. psychological hazards

2. Establish a hazard identification team by including both managerial and non-managerial workers with multi-disciplinary expertise
3. Conduct a hazard identification process and establish lists of potential hazards specific to each location, procedure, activity, and equipment
4. Review previous incidents and risk assessments
5. Review regulatory requirements
6. Record and communicate identified hazards to relevant interested parties
7. Regularly review the effectiveness of hazard identification processes

Auditors Will Check That

- Processes have been defined for hazard identification and their effectiveness.
- Factors such as routine and non-routine activities, human factors, new or changed hazards, potential emergency situations, affected people, changes to knowledge and information, and psychological hazards have been considered in hazard identification procedures.
- Previous incidents and legal requirements have been considered in hazard identification procedures.
- Relevant interested parties are aware of potential hazards in their work area.

Records

- Hazard identification process (non-mandatory), including:

  * authorities and responsibilities
  * hazard identification methodology
  * hazard identification committee
  * hazard identification criteria
  * locations, procedures, and activities to be reviewed
  * frequency of hazard identification processes

- List of potential hazards (non-mandatory), including:

  * location
  * possible hazard
  * type of hazard
  * identification tool (e.g. inspections, internal audits)
  * affected people (e.g. workers, contractors, visitors)
  * control measures
  * responsibility
  * target date

6.1.2.2 *Assessment of OHS Risks*

Risk is the effect of uncertainty, which can influence the organisation in a positive or negative way. Organisations should establish, implement, and maintain processes to assess OHS and other risks. In terms of hazard management, a risk is a chance (great or small) that someone will be harmed by a hazard. After identifying potential hazards, organisations should assess the likelihood of occurrence and the severity of injury or ill health that can be caused by hazards to determine which hazards carry the most risk.

Organisations should also consider other risks that could come from the internal and external issues identified in clause 4, from changes in the legal requirements or the needs of interested parties. Thus, organisations should establish, implement, and maintain a process to:

a. assess OHS risks from the identified hazards while taking into account the effectiveness of existing controls
b. determine and assess other risks related to the establishment, implementation, operation, and maintenance of the OHSMS

Risk assessment is a process of evaluating the risks arising from hazards, taking into account the adequacy of any existing controls, and deciding whether the level of risk is acceptable. An acceptable risk is a risk that has been reduced to a level that the organisation is willing to assume with respect to its legal obligation, OHS policy, and objectives.

An organisation's methodology for risk assessment should be established by considering the scope and nature of the business to ensure that the process is proactive. A common four-step risk assessment methodology based on a five-by-five matrix is demonstrated in Figure 6.1:

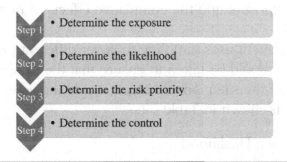

Step 1 • Determine the exposure
Step 2 • Determine the likelihood
Step 3 • Determine the risk priority
Step 4 • Determine the control

Figure 6.1   Four-step risk assessment methodology (ISO 31010:2020).

Step 1: Determine the Exposure

The first step is to determine the severity and consequences of the identified hazard. If rating scales are being used, it is highly important that the descriptive scales of likelihood and severity are clearly defined to ensure that different individuals interpret them consistently. Risk assessments to evaluate the harm from exposure to chemical, biological, and physical agents

Table 6.1 Five-Level Severity Scale

A. SEVERITY	
Descriptor	*Definition*
5	Fatality or permanent disability; very serious financial loss of more than $100,000
4	Serious injury or long-term illness—more than 31 calendar days' absence from work; serious financial loss of more than $10,000 and less than $100,000
3	Significant injury or illness—more than 7 days & less than 31 calendar days' absence from work; significant financial loss of more than $1,000 and less than $10,000
2	Moderate injury or illness—less than 7 calendar days' absence from work; moderate financial loss of more than $100 and less than $1,000
1	Minor injury or illness—first aid needed; no time lost; minor financial loss of less than $100

may require measurement of exposure concentrations using appropriate instruments and sampling methods. These concentrations are compared to applicable occupational exposure limits or standards. Organisations should ensure that the risk assessment considers both the short-term and long-term consequences of exposure and the cumulative effects of multiple agents and exposures.

When risk assessment uses sampling to cover different locations or situations, proper care should be taken to ensure that the samples used adequately represent all the situations and locations being assessed. An example of a severity scale is shown in Table 6.1.

Step 2: Determine the Likelihood

The second step is to determine the probability of an occurrence of the hazard. Hazards that could cause harm to a large number of people should be given careful consideration even when they are less likely to occur. Risks to sensitive populations (e.g. pregnant workers) and vulnerable groups (e.g. inexperienced workers) as well as any particular susceptibilities of the individuals involved in performing particular tasks (e.g. the ability of an individual who is colour-blind to read instructions) should also be carefully considered. An example of a likelihood scale is shown in Table 6.2.

Table 6.2   Five-Level Likelihood Scale

B. LIKELIHOOD		
Descriptor	*Definition*	*Probability*
5	Almost certain; expected in most circumstances	91–100%
4	Very likely; will probably occur in most circumstances	61–90%
3	Likely; might occur at some time	41–60%
2	Unlikely; could occur at some time	10–40%
1	Very unlikely; may occur only in exceptional circumstances	0–10%

Step 3: Determine the Risk Priority

Priority is the combination of exposure and likelihood. Prioritising hazards is one way to help determine which risk is the most serious and needs to be controlled first. There are several ways to determine the level of risk (refer to ISO 31010:2019). An example of a common five-by-five risk priority matrix is demonstrated in Table 6.3.

Step 4: Determine the Control

Once organisations have established the priorities, they can decide on ways to control each specific hazard. Risk control methods are often grouped into the following categories:

- ■ *Avoidance*: change the plan to eliminate the threat. Refuse to accept the risk (e.g. get rid of a dangerous machine)
- ■ *Reduction*: reduce the likelihood or consequences of the risk (e.g. replace the machine with a safer version)
- ■ *Retention*: accept the risk and exposure with no further action to manage—often for low risks (e.g. a smoke detector alarm which has a 0.0001% margin of error)
- ■ *Transfer*: shift responsibility and consequences to another party, though the risk still exists (e.g. public and product liability insurance)

If the organisation has determined to do something about a risk, then they need to plan their actions by defining what actions are required, who is responsible for this risk, the target completion date, required resources, and the frequency of the process to be reviewed.

Table 6.3   Five-by-Five Risk Priority Matrix

C. RISK PRIORITY						
		A. SEVERITY				
		5	4	3	2	1
B. Likelihood	5	25	20	15	10	5
	4	20	16	12	8	4
	3	15	12	9	6	3
	2	10	8	6	4	2
	1	5	4	3	2	1
Risk	Risk Rating					
15–25	High priority for risk elimination, or control without delay. *Do not proceed.* Requires immediate attention. Introduce further high-level controls to lower the risk level. Reassess before proceeding.					
5–14	Medium priority for risk elimination, or control as soon as possible. *Review before commencing work.* Introduce new controls and/or maintain high-level controls to lower the risk level. Monitor frequently to ensure control measures are working.					
1–4	Low priority for risk elimination, or control after higher risks have been addressed. *Record and monitor.* Proceed with work. Review regularly if any equipment/people/materials/work processes or procedures change.					

If the risk cannot be eliminated, organisations should have a plan to deal with the situations that may arise because of the risk, including defining what emergency plans are required, identifying training needed for workers to be able to deal with the potential emergency, identifying the resources required, and designating responsibility for communicating on and managing the potential emergency.

When determining controls for potential hazards and risks, it is essential to consider the following hierarchy of controls (which will be discussed further in Chapter 8):

■ *Highest level*: eliminate a hazard
■ *Fourth level*: substitute less hazardous processes

- *Third level:* engage engineering controls
- *Second level:* use administrative controls and training
- *Lowest level:* employ the use of personal protective equipment (PPE)

Steps to Complete

1. Determine a process for risk assessment including methodology and criteria for the evaluation of risks with respect to their:

   a. scope
   b. nature
   c. timing, to ensure proactive measures

2. Establish competent risk assessment teams by including both managerial and non-managerial workers with multi-disciplinary expertise.
3. Identify potential risks arising from hazards, and other risks relevant to the OHSMS.
4. Determine the level of exposure.
5. Determine the likelihood of occurrence.
6. Determine the risk priority.
7. Determine the control measures needed to be applied.
8. Identify required resources.
9. Allocate the responsible person/department to the risk.
10. Plan and implement control measures.
11. Verify, validate risk assessment processes.
12. Document and communicate risk assessment processes.
13. Regularly review the effectiveness of risk assessment processes.

Auditors Will Check That

- Processes that have been defined for risk assessment and their effectiveness.
- Risk assessment teams are competent.
- Risk assessment methodology is consistent throughout the organisation to avoid confusion and has been properly understood by the relevant interested parties.
- The hierarchy of controls has been considered when determining the control measures.
- The organisation has considered risks other than OHS specific risks (e.g. not enough support from top management, lack of motivation, not enough resources, too complicated OHSMS).

Records

■ Risk assessment process (mandatory)

  * risk assessment methodology
  * risk assessment criteria
  * risk assessment committee

■ Risk and opportunity assessment records (mandatory)

  * risk and opportunity type (e.g. OHS hazards, legal requirement, external issues, interested parties)
  * risk description
  * risk severity
  * risk probability
  * risk rating
  * responsible person
  * treatment type
  * actions proposed
  * resources required
  * proposed completion date
  * proposed review date
  * actual actions taken to address the risk
  * review of the effectiveness of actions taken

6.1.2.3   *Assessment of OHS Opportunities*

As previously discussed, risks can have positive or negative consequences which can expose the organisation to an opportunity, a threat, or both (ISO 31001:2018). Therefore, in addition to the negative impacts of risks, the standard requires identification and assessment of the OHS and other opportunities to improve the health and safety performance of the organisation. When determining opportunities, organisations may consider potential benefits and resources required as criteria to prioritise opportunities. Examples of OHS opportunities include:

■ Conducting regular OHS committee meetings
■ Performing job hazard analysis
■ Using a work permit system for hazardous activities
■ Finding ways to reduce work monotony
■ Conducting an ergonomic assessment of workplaces

■ Using new technologies to improve health and safety in the workplace
■ Improving the health and safety culture of the organisation by providing training to relevant individuals

Steps to Complete

1. Determine a process to identify opportunities that can enhance the organisations' performance.
2. Establish methodology and criteria to effectively identify and prioritise opportunities.
3. Appoint a competent team.
4. Conduct an opportunity assessment to identify processes for improvement such as:

   a. conducting frequent risk and hazard assessment meetings
   b. providing training on root cause analysis
   c. regular reviewing of the effectiveness of existing controls
   d. receiving suggestions from non-managerial workers
   e. providing counselling and support to workers
   f. encouraging the reporting of potential hazards and near misses

5. Allocate resources and implement identified opportunities.
6. Document and communicate opportunity assessment results.

Auditors Will Check That

■ OHS opportunities and other opportunities are being assessed.
■ Identified opportunities are addressed properly.
■ Non-managerial workers are involved in the opportunity assessment processes.

Records

■ Process for assessment of OHS opportunities and other opportunities for the OHSMS (mandatory)
■ OHS opportunity assessment records (mandatory), including:

   * identification of opportunities to adapt the work environment to workers, eliminate hazards, and reduce OHS risks
   * plan of action to address identified opportunities
   * list of responsibilities
   * list of required resources

* record of actions taken to address the opportunity
* review of effectiveness of actions taken

6.1.3   Determination of Legal Requirements

Obligations arising from mandatory and voluntary commitments are risks and opportunities to the organisation and should be managed properly. The standard requires organisations to establish, implement, and maintain a process for identifying, complying with, and reviewing the legal and other requirements applicable to the organisation. This is a key factor in the success of the OHSMS. There are some mandatory requirements that the organisation should comply with such as:

■ laws and regulations
■ permits, licences, or other forms of authorisation
■ orders, rules, or guidance issued by regulatory agencies
■ judgments of courts or administrative tribunals
■ treaties, conventions, and protocols

But compliance obligation can also include requirements from other interested parties related to the OHS, which the organisation chooses to adopt, such as:

■ Agreements with community groups or non-governmental entities
■ Agreements with public authorities and customers
■ Organisational requirements
■ Voluntary principles or codes of practice
■ Voluntary labelling or health and safety commitments
■ Obligations arising under contractual arrangements with other organisations
■ Relevant organisational and industry standards

Organisations should identify what requirements are applicable to them. Each country has its specific laws and regulations. Thus, it is highly recommended that the organisation gets advice about the necessary legal requirements from legal or other specialised experts. However, ultimately organisations cannot outsource the responsibility to other parties.

   Organisations should define a process to ensure that they have access to the latest version of the requirements. Organisations may find OHS regulations on the website of the relevant government agencies. It is also recommended that organisations are registered to receive the governmental agencies' newsletters, to be informed about any changes in the requirements.

So that organisations can determine what they need to do to comply with the requirements, it would be beneficial to allocate a person or department responsible for ensuring that the requirements are reviewed regularly and progress is monitored. This person/department should be tasked with informing the management team of any changes to the requirements relevant to their industry's functions.

It is highly important to define a process for communicating the relevant requirements to all interested parties within and outside the organisation. Organisations should maintain and retain documented information on legal and other requirements to ensure that they are updated and continually reviewed.

Steps to Complete

1. Establish a team comprising competent individuals to actively identify applicable legal and other requirements.
2. Determine a process to identify and comply with legal and other requirements.
3. Determine how to maintain access to up-to-date legal and other requirements.
4. Determine how these requirements apply to the organisation, how to comply, and what needs to be communicated internally and externally.
5. Determine whether the organisation is compliant with the requirements.
6. If not compliant, determine what needs to be done.
7. Assign a competent person/department to manage the requirements.
8. Document and communicate applicable legal and other requirements.
9. Regularly review and update applicable requirements.

Auditors Will Check That

- There is an effective process in place to identify applicable legal and other requirements.
- There is a process for the organisation to get access to the latest updates of the legal and other requirements.
- The organisation can determine when, how, and to whom the legal and other requirements should be communicated.

Records

- Process for determination of legal and other requirements (non-mandatory)
- Legal and other obligations register (mandatory), documenting:

  * compliance obligation type (statutory, regulatory, standard, contractual, voluntary)
  * requirement title
  * latest version number
  * applicable section
  * consequences of non-compliance
  * hyperlink
  * compliance status
  * responsible person
  * review frequency
  * last review date

6.1.4 *Planning Action*

After identifying hazards, risks, opportunities, legal, and other requirements, organisations should have adequate measures to effectively control and respond to such situations in their early planning stages. The standard requires organisations to plan to address:

- Hazards, risks, and opportunities
- Legal and other requirements
- Emergency situations
- Integration of actions to OHSMS and other organisation processes
- Effectiveness of actions taken

Addressing hazards, risks, and opportunities can take the form of OHS control measures. While determining controls needed, organisations should consider the hierarchy of controls, which will be explained in Chapter 8 (clause 8.1.2).

Planning to address legal and other requirements is highly interdependent on proper identification of the required level of compliance with applicable laws and other obligations. When planning to address legal and other requirements, organisations should determine processes to:

- Ensure access to the latest legal and other requirements.
- Achieve and maintain compliance with the applicable legal and other requirements.

- Define OHS objectives to accomplish required obligations.
- Allocate responsibilities, resources, and a timeframe to achieve legal and other requirements.
- Regularly monitor and measure compliance with legal and other obligations.

Organisations should also define plans to respond to emergency situations, as detailed in Chapter 8 (clause 8.2). Emergency situations are unexpected events that require an immediate response to minimise any adverse effects on the health and safety of workers and other relevant interested parties. Emergency situations can originate within or outside the organisation.

Organisations should plan to identify potential emergency situations and be prepared to respond to such situations. An emergency response plan can include establishing emergency procedures, providing emergency response training to workers, assigning emergency response teams such as first-aiders and fire wardens, supplying adequate emergency equipment and facilities, conducting regular emergency drills, and communicating with emergency services.

Hazards, risks, opportunities, legal requirements, and emergency situations planned for in this clause are linked to other processes of the organisation. For instance, the determination of applicable legal requirements will be effective when completed by a competent team of experts and needs to be integrated with the competency and training functions of the organisation. Another example is that hazards, risks, and opportunities will be effectively managed only if they are properly communicated with workers at all levels, and this needs to be integrated with procedures for the consultation and participation of workers. Therefore, when planning actions for these situations, organisations should integrate them with other business processes and regularly review their effectiveness.

Steps to Complete

1. To address hazards, risks, and opportunities:

   a. identify hazards, risks, and opportunities
   b. define controls needed to manage hazards, risks, and opportunities by considering the hierarchy of controls in planning
   c. define responsible persons to manage and communicate hazards, risks, opportunities, legal and other requirements, and emergency situations

d. define resources required

e. define required completion date

f. define a process to measure and monitor the effectiveness of plans and controls

g. define review frequency

2. To address legal and other requirements:

a. identify legal and other requirements

b. determine actions required to comply with the legal and other requirements

c. define responsible persons to manage and communicate legal and other requirements

d. define resources required

e. define required completion date

f. define a process to measure and monitor the compliance of the organisation with its legal and other requirements

g. define review frequency

3. To address emergency situations:

a. identify potential emergency situations

b. define controls needed to manage emergency situations by considering the hierarchy of controls in planning

c. prepare emergency procedures

d. define resources required

e. define proper emergency assembly points and exits

f. provide emergency equipment and facilities

g. provide emergency training to all personnel

h. establish an emergency response team to manage and communicate emergency situations within and outside the organisation

i. review the effectiveness of emergency plans by having drills to simulate various emergency situations

j. communicate and provide relevant information to all workers, contractors, visitors, government bodies, emergency response services, and, where appropriate, the local community

4. Determine approaches to integrate planned actions with the OHSMS and other business processes. This can be discussed in management reviews, OHS committee meetings, toolbox talks, and other formal and informal meetings.

5. Regularly evaluate the effectiveness of the actions taken, which can be done through audits, inspections, and other OHS performance assessment methods.

Auditors Will Check That

■ The organisation has planned actions to address hazards, risks, opportunities, legal requirements, and emergency situations.
■ The organisation has a process to determine the controls required for these situations.
■ The organisation has defined how and by whom these controls should be applied.
■ The organisation has a plan to integrate its OHS processes into other business processes.
■ The organisation has a process to evaluate the effectiveness of these integrations.

Records

■ List of potential hazards, risks, opportunities, legal, and other requirements, and emergency situations (mandatory), including:

  * control measures considering the hierarchy of controls
  * impact on other business processes
  * required resources
  * target date
  * monitoring methodology
  * monitoring frequency

■ Records of actual actions taken to apply controls (non-mandatory)
■ Records of reviews of the effectiveness of control measures (non-mandatory)

6.2 OHS Objectives and Planning to Achieve Them

Clause 6.2.1 (OHS objectives) of the standard requires organisations to establish objectives to maintain and continually improve the OHSMS performance. The term 'maintain' has been used in this clause to emphasise that if a certain level of performance on an objective has been achieved and it has been decided that no further improvement is required at that stage, organisations can set an objective to 'maintain' the newly achieved performance level. However, as the standard follows a PDCA cycle, it is important to note that regardless of size, complexity, and maturity of the organisation, there are always areas for improvement.

When defining the OHS objectives, organisations should consider the context of the organisation, its OHS policy, legal and other obligations, the results of consultation with and participation of workers, identified hazards, risks, opportunities, emergency situations, and nonconformances, including feedback from interested parties related to the improvement of OHS performance. Defined objectives should be SMART. Typical examples of OHS objectives are to:

■ Achieve a 20% reduction in hand injury incidents while working with a specific machine.
■ Introduce controls for the top two health hazards in a department.
■ Eliminate a hazardous substance from a process.
■ Increase the OHS training budget by 20%.
■ Reduce the noise level of the workshop by 20 dBA within a year.
■ Comply with a legal requirement within six months.

Once OHS objectives have been defined, organisations should communicate these objectives to relevant interested parties to enhance the commitment to health and safety and make clear what the organisation is trying to achieve through its OHSMS. Constructive objectives can improve OHS performance, while poorly determined objectives may cause failure or waste resources. Thus, organisations should regularly measure the effectiveness of the objectives and update them as appropriate.

For objectives to be successfully accomplished, organisations need to clearly specify the methods and implementation processes required to achieve them. In clause 6.2.2 (Planning to achieve OHS objectives), the standard requires organisations to consider the following when planning to achieve their OHS objectives:

■ Processes, activities, and tasks needed to be done
■ Resources required (e.g. financial, human, infrastructure, equipment)
■ Responsible persons
■ Timeframe
■ Process to monitor the progress and evaluate the results to ensure that OHS objectives have been achieved—this can be an important input for MRMs

■ Determine how the actions to achieve the objectives can be embedded in other business and OHSMS processes

A helpful tool to monitor the achievement of OHS objectives is the use of key performance indicators (KPIs). KPIs are measurable representations of the progress towards an intended result. Organisations can allocate one or more performance indicators to each OHS objective. Examples of these KPIs are:

■ Number of OHS incidents and near misses within the last six months
■ Number of MRMs or toolbox talks conducted in the second quarter of the year
■ Amount of budget allocated to the OHS training last year
■ Number of conducted OHS audits versus number of planned OHS audits

Organisations are required to maintain and retain documented information on their OHS objectives and plans to achieve them.

Steps to Complete

1. Conduct meetings to establish OHS objectives and plans to achieve them. Attendees can be top management, managerial and non-managerial workers, and workers' representatives. The agenda of such meetings may include:

   a. determining OHS objectives
   b. defining tasks to be completed to achieve objectives
   c. identifying resources required
   d. assigning responsible person/department
   e. defining target dates
   f. determining monitoring methodology and frequency
   g. assigning responsible person(s) to objectively review progress

2. Communicate OHS objectives to interested parties including workers and contractors.
3. Regularly monitor the progress of the OHS objectives, identify issues, and update objectives where appropriate.

Auditors Will Check

■ The annual OHS objectives of the organisation
■ That these objectives are measurable
■ How the organisation will ensure the defined objectives are achievable

- That the organisation has established plans to achieve its OHS objectives
- That adequate resources are allocated to achieve each objective
- How the organisation monitors the progress of its OHS objectives
- What the organisation's processes are for determining new OHS objectives
- How workers have participated in identifying and establishing OHS objectives

Records

- List of OHS objectives and plans to achieve them (mandatory), including:

  * objective description
  * required resources
  * responsibility
  * target date
  * monitoring methodology
  * monitoring frequency

Chapter 7

Support

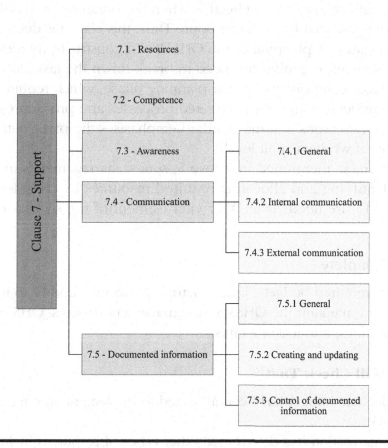

Overview of Clause 7—Support (ISO 45001:2018).

Having the right resources is a key factor in the successful implementation of the OHSMS. Resources can include finance, human, infrastructure, equipment, machinery, new procedures, external consultancy, technology,

DOI: 10.4324/9781003266532-7

training, and awareness. The ISO 45001 standard provides guidance on how to identify resources, determine competence, raise awareness, and document required information.

7.1   Resources

Organisations should determine what resources are required to effectively establish, implement, maintain, and continually improve their OHSMS and then define how these resources will be supplied. Identifying and allocating resources are an ongoing process since the OHS requirements may change over time.

Resource allocation will be effective when the organisation has a clear understanding of what needs to be done. Thus, this clause is deeply inter-linked with clause 6: planning of the OHSMS. To constructively identify required resources, organisations need to break down the tasks into smaller and deliverable components in their planning phase, which requires a comprehensive understanding of the targeted processes and procedures. This is one of many reasons that the standard emphasises the participation and consultation of workers at all levels.

In addition, as mentioned in clause 5, senior management's involvement in identifying and allocating required resources by considering current and future needs is another vital element of the success of the OHSMS.

Steps to Complete

- Review required budgets, infrastructure, personnel, and IT to implement and maintain the OHSMS in management reviews, OHS committee meetings, and toolbox talks.

Auditors Will Check That

- An adequate budget has been allocated to implement an effective OHSMS
- The organisation has determined other types of resources including competent personnel, infrastructure, and IT
- Top management was involved in determining required resources
- Non-managerial workers and workers reps were consulted before making decisions about required resources.

Records

■ Evidence of evaluation and allocation of resources to the OHS operations that can be ascertained through MRM minutes, toolbox talks, and OHS committee meetings (non-mandatory).

7.2 Competence

Workers play a key role in establishing, implementing, maintaining, and continually improving an organisation's OHSMS. Therefore, they should be competent to effectively perform their OHS responsibilities. The standard emphasises determining the competence of all workers operating under the organisation's control to carry out their OHS responsibilities.

Workers are considered competent if they have the required level of knowledge, skill, and experience to complete their assigned tasks in a safe and healthy manner. To determine the competency of workers, organisations should:

1. Define the competencies required for the roles that can affect OHSMS and its performance. Required competencies can be education, qualifications, and experience—operational or technical. It is crucial that all workers have the required ability to identify hazards and manage OHS risks associated with their work activities. Special consideration should be given when defining ideal competence for workers conducting hazard and risk assessments, audits, incident investigations, and tasks associated with significant hazards and risks.
2. Ensure that workers at all levels have the necessary competence for their OHS responsibilities.
3. Determine actions required for workers to acquire the necessary competence, if they are deemed to not meet the required level of competency. These actions can include training, refresher courses, hiring competent workers, or contracting of external expertise.

Organisations should consider the following factors when determining the ideal competence levels of workers' roles:

■ Education, qualifications, and experience required to undertake the role effectively
■ The working environment

- The OHS policy
- Legal and other requirements
- Control measures from hazard and risks assessments
- Participation and consultation of workers
- Potential context or work changes

Organisations should encourage workers to participate in ascertaining the competence needed for their roles. Training options may include gaining experience by working under the supervision of more experienced workers, formal training including classroom sessions and instructions, or training provided by external consultants.

Training is generally an expensive solution for the organisation. Thus, when competence is acquired through training, the organisation should define a process to document, and monitor and evaluate its effectiveness to ensure that the conducted training is adding value to the organisation's OHS performance. The effectiveness of training can be evaluated through exams, tests, on-the-job monitoring by more experienced workers, and so on.

In addition to role-based training, organisations should also consider training that is relevant to all workers, such as hazard and risk identification training, use of firefighting equipment, emergency response training, and general health and safety instructions.

When determining the required training, heads of departments, supervisors, workers, and workers' representatives should be consulted to ensure that the designated training accurately represents the knowledge and skills required to perform their assigned OHS tasks.

Organisations should pay particular attention to the competency of workers who undertake responsibilities for OHS legal requirements, such as first-aiders, fire wardens, and OHS representatives, where applicable.

If supplying of workers is being managed by a contractor, the organisation should have adequate internal evaluation systems in place to verify the workers' competency and suitability before and during the work and issue work permits to competent external workers (a sample work permit can be found in Appendix D).

Competency is subject to the process and technology being used. Therefore, organisations should establish a process to regularly review the ideal competencies and reassess the competence level of their workers.

Organisations should retain documented information as evidence of their actions to ensure the competency of their workers. This documented information may include competence evaluation procedures, role-based ideal competencies, records of assessment of competence, training plans, records of training, and evaluation of the effectiveness of trainings.

Steps to Complete

1. Define competence criteria for the roles that affect the OHS performance of the organisation. Examples of ideal OHS competence are:

   * the capability to identify potential hazards and risks in the workplace
   * adequate training and experience in using forklifts in a safe manner
   * understanding of how to perform cutting/welding in a manner to ensure the safety and health of the worker and others in the workplace
   * a valid first aid or fire warden certificate
   * familiarity with the legal requirements relating to working at heights

2. Evaluate workers' competence levels against identified criteria.
3. Define an appropriate plan to fill the identified gaps between actual and ideal competence levels. This can be done either by providing required training to existing workers or by hiring competent personnel. A training plan should include refresher training and training for new technology, or changes in equipment and processes.
4. Evaluate the effectiveness of the training provided through exams, tests, or on-the-job monitoring by more experienced workers.
5. Maintain a list of competent workers to ensure that specific OHS tasks are only carried out by competent workers.
6. Regularly re-evaluate ideal competence and the competence levels of workers.
7. Keep records of the previous steps.

Auditors Will Check That

■ Ideal competence levels for the roles that can affect OHS performance have been determined.
■ Definitions of ideal competencies are consistent with the nature of the roles related to the OHS performance.
■ Gaps between ideal and actual competence have been identified.
■ A training plan/matrix is available.
■ Workers have been consulted about the training they require.

Records

■ Ideal competence (non-mandatory)

* role and designation
* competence type (education, experience, operational, technical)
* description of competence
* ideal level of competency

■ Competence evaluation (mandatory)

* role and designation
* competence type (education, experience, functional, operational, technical)
* description of competence
* ideal level of competency
* current level of competence
* training required

■ Competency matrix linked to employee's job description (non-mandatory)
■ Training records (non-mandatory)

* training topic
* training type (classroom, online, on the job)
* trainer
* training date
* trainee name
* pre-training competence level
* evaluation methodology
* evaluator
* post-training competence level
* evaluation date
* signatory

7.3 Awareness

To effectively contribute to the achievement of the OHS objectives, workers should be aware of the organisation's health and safety procedures relevant to their tasks. Thus, the standard requires organisations to provide awareness training to inform workers performing tasks under the organisation's control about what they need to do to support the OHSMS. Organisations should decide what information to disseminate, how, when and to whom. However, there are the following six main topics that ISO 45001 defines as necessary to communicate to workers:

1. OHS policy and objectives to ensure that workers are aware of the organisation's goals for health and safety in the workplace.
2. Identification of workers' contribution to the OHSMS, to ensure that workers are aware of how improved OHS performance could benefit them in terms of reducing chances of injury and ill health.
3. Potential consequences of not conforming to the OHSMS requirements, including injury and ill health that may be caused by deviation from OHS policies and procedures.
4. Previous incidents and outcomes of investigations that are relevant to them and can affect how they do their job to prevent recurrence of similar hazardous situations.
5. Hazards and risks associated with their roles and how their behaviour can affect these hazards and risks.
6. Understanding that they can and should stop working if their health and safety is in imminent and serious danger and that they will be protected from undue consequences for doing so.

These topics can be covered through induction training, specific training, or toolbox talks. Awareness training can consist of short sessions supplemented with videos and demonstrations of the key elements of the OHS issues. Posters, newsletters, and bulletin boards are other methods of promoting health and safety awareness.

When presenting these awareness topics, organisations should take into account the abilities, languages, skills, and literacy levels of the workers to ensure that they clearly understand what is being presented to them. Furthermore, contractors, sub-contractors, and agency staff, as well as visitors, are also required to be made aware of all the potential OHS hazards and risks they may be exposed to in that workplace.

Steps to Complete

1. Include the following topics in the organisation's induction programme:

    a. OHS policy and objectives
    b. benefits of OHSMS and workers' OHS roles and responsibilities
    c. consequences of not conforming to the OHSMS requirements

    d. maintenance of a hazard and OHS risk register relevant to their duties and work area

    e. a clear statement from the organisation confirming that workers will be protected from any consequences if they remove themselves from work situations that can present a serious and imminent danger to their health and safety

2. Include the following in toolbox talks, OHS committee meetings, or other OHS meetings:

    a. any updates in OHS policy and objectives

    b. any updates in hazard and OHS risk register

    c. incidents and outcomes of investigations that are relevant to workers

Auditors Will Check That

■ The organisation has a system for communicating OHS policy and objectives to workers, contractors, sub-contractors, visitors, suppliers, etc.

■ Workers are aware of the benefits of OHSMS and their responsibility to positively contribute to it.

■ Workers have received training on potential hazards and risks in their work area.

■ The organisation has a process to ensure workers are allowed to stop working if they determine that their work situation is not safe.

■ Workers are aware of the consequences of not conforming to the OHSMS requirements.

Records

■ Minutes of health and safety meetings (e.g. OHS induction training, toolbox talks) with workers, with the following agenda items:

    * OHS policy and objectives

    * potential hazards and risks in the workplace

    * process for reporting hazards, risks, and incidents

    * importance of OHSMS and consequences of nonconformity

    * incidents, and outcomes of the investigations

    * emphasis from the organisation that it will support voluntary removal from work if the situation presents a serious and imminent danger to the worker's health and safety

7.4 Communication

Poor communication is one of the main causes of incidents, stress, frustration, and confusion in an organisation and often leads to workers not being motivated or inspired to collaborate. Failure to inform operational workers and on-site contractors about a potential hazard can cause serious health and safety incidents.

Most successful businesses already have well-established systems for communication internally and externally. However, the standard requires organisations to determine effective processes for internal and external communications that are relevant to the OHSMS. When defining communication processes relevant to their OHSMS, organisations should consider:

- What needs to be communicated
- When it needs to be communicated
- Who needs to see the communication
- How it should be communicated

Subjects that can trigger communication may include:

- Communicating OHS policy and objectives to interested parties
- Communicating results of OHS committee meetings
- Reporting results of incident investigations to relevant interested parties
- Communicating with regulatory bodies and authorities to access applicable laws and responses regarding OHS legal compliance status
- Informing relevant workers and contractors about hazards and risks in the working area
- Communicating with management team and workers about OHS concerns and OFIs

Organisations also need to define *when* particular communications relevant to the OHSMS should be carried out. The frequency and timing of the communication can be affected by factors such as:

- Changes in the OHS policy, objectives, and procedures
- Changes in laws, regulation, and compliance status
- New decisions from the management team relevant to the OHSMS
- New hazards and risks identified
- New workers and contractors employed
- New equipment and tools added to the workplace

When determining *how* to communicate, organisations should take into account aspects such as the language, culture, and literacy of their workforce. Organisations should also consider the level of detail that needs to be communicated. Generally, middle to lower managers and technical staff require more detailed information, whereas higher management and lower-level workers may need only a summary.

Communication can be done verbally (e.g. briefing, meeting) or by formal memorandums, newsletters, posters and leaflets, or via a suggestion box. Examples of common modes of communication are:

- Printed reports of OHS performance for MRMs
- Hazards and risk assessments displayed on noticeboards
- Group meetings or briefings on how to use a machine in the workshop
- Emails sent to authorities and regulatory bodies asking for the latest version of legal requirements
- Signs displayed on the organisation's premises.

The standard categorises communication into two areas of internal and external communication. Internally, organisations are required to establish a two-way communication process to enable workers at all levels and functions to receive information relevant to the OHSMS and contribute to its continual improvement. Examples of internal communications include:

- Top management distributing roles and responsibilities and receiving feedback to ensure that defined responsibilities are within the workers' control
- A system to report hazards, risks, opportunities, and suggestions
- OHS policy being disseminated throughout the organisation
- Workers contributing to defining OHS objectives and being advised of the actions required to achieve them
- Notice of changes to OHS procedures and policies
- Incident investigations and their results

Organisations should take particular care when dealing with communications from external parties including enforcement authorities and contractors. Externally, organisations are required to establish a process to communicate information relevant to their OHSMS and as required by its compliance obligations. Organisations should identify the necessary external communications that are required for the effective operation of their OHSMS.

Organisations should also define the level of OHS communication needed with their external parties to meet their specific requirements. The mode of communication with external parties largely depends on the level of obligation that the organisation is required to comply with and the risks they may face. Examples of external communication include:

■ Publishing OHS policy on the organisation's website
■ Submitting results of audits or incident investigations to authorities
■ Requesting latest versions of OHS acts and codes of practice from regulatory bodies
■ Informing authorities about an emergency situation
■ Providing information about OHS processes, emergency evacuation arrangements, and OHS protocols to visitors and contractors at the worksite

Organisations should maintain and retain documented information as evidence of their communications.

A sample OHS-related communication procedure can be found in Appendix E.

Steps to Complete

1. Determine a process for internal and external communication, by establishing:

   a. what to communicate
   b. when to communicate
   c. to whom to communicate
   d. how to communicate

2. Define the roles and responsibilities of the people implementing this process.
3. Review the effectiveness of internal and external communications by top management.

Auditor Will Check That

■ The organisation has established a communication process.
■ The organisation communicates essential health and safety information to its interested parties.
■ The organisation has a system for receiving and responding to communications with an external origin such as regulatory bodies and contractors.

Records

■ Internal and external communication procedures (non-mandatory):

  * authorities and responsibilities
  * communication methodology

    ▪ what will be communicated
    ▪ when to communicate
    ▪ to whom to communicate
    ▪ how to communicate

■ Evidence of internal and external communications relevant to health and safety (mandatory). Examples of this communication may include:

  * communication from top management to managerial and non-managerial workers
  * communication from managerial and non-managerial workers to top management
  * communication with regulatory bodies
  * communication with contractors, sub-contractors, and suppliers

7.5   Documented Information

Documented information includes 'documented procedures' and 'records' that have been used in earlier versions of standards (OHSAS 18001 spoke of the need to "document and record"). ISO 45001 refers to 'documented procedures' as documents that need to be 'maintained' and 'records' as documents that need to be 'retained.'

Policies, objectives, standard operating procedures (SOPs), site-specific safety plans (SSSPs), work instructions, regulatory requirements, and other documents providing OHS information that needs to be updated and kept current are examples of documents that need to be 'maintained' by the organisation.

Meeting minutes, audit reports, lists of potential hazards, results of the calibration of measuring equipment, licences, and other documents that provide evidence and results of actions taken are examples of documents that need to be 'retained' by the organisation.

Having more documented information than required is a common mistake that many organisations make. Organisations should determine the level of documented information necessary to control their OHSMS and not beyond that. Organisations need to maintain and retain documented information which is:

■ A mandatory requirement of ISO 45001
■ Required by the organisation to effectively manage their OHSMS

Modes of documented information can include operational procedures, work instructions, reports, slides, flow charts, posters, signs, and emails.

There are 20 mandatory documents for ISO 45001 as shown in Table 7.1.

Table 7.1   ISO 45001:2018 Mandatory Documented Information (ISO 45001:2018)

No.	ISO 45001 Clause	Required Documented Information
1	4.3	The scope of the OHSMS
2	5.2	OHS policy
3	5.3	Responsibilities and authorities for relevant roles within the OHSMS as assigned and communicated at all levels within the organisation
4	6.1.1	The organisation's OHS risks and opportunities that need to be addressed
5	6.1.1	The organisation's processes needed for actions to address risks and opportunities (clause 6.1), to the extent necessary to have confidence they are carried out as planned
6	6.1.2.2	The methodology(ies) and criteria used for the assessment of OHS risks and other risks to the OHSMS
7	6.1.3	The organisation's legal requirements and other requirements (to be kept updated to reflect any changes)
8	6.2.2	OHS objectives and plans to achieve them
9	7.2	Appropriate documented information as evidence of competence of personnel
10	7.4.1	Appropriate documented information as evidence of organisation's communications related to OHS management

Table 7.1 *(Continued)* **ISO 45001:2018 Mandatory Documented Information (ISO 45001:2018)**

No.	ISO 45001 Clause	Required Documented Information
11	8.1.1	Documented information (to the extent necessary) to have confidence that the processes have been carried out as planned
12	8.2	Documented information on the process(es) and on the plans for responding to potential emergency situations
13	9.1.1	Documented information as the evidence of the results of monitoring, measurement, analysis, and evaluation
14	9.1.1	Documented information on the maintenance, calibration, or verification of measuring equipment
15	9.1.2	Documented information of the compliance evaluation result(s)
16	9.2.2	Documented information as evidence of the implementation of the audit programme and the audit results
17	9.3	Documented information as evidence of the results of management reviews
18	10.2	Documented information as evidence of the nature of the incidents or nonconformities and any subsequent actions taken
19	10.2	Documented information as evidence of the results of any action and corrective action, including their effectiveness
20	10.3	Documented information as evidence of continual improvement

Depending on organisational factors such as size, complexity, legal requirements, and competency requirements, organisations may consider maintaining and retaining other documented information to control their OHSMS performance. For instance, if a procedure causes misunderstanding and misinterpretation for existing and new workers (or other interested parties) leading to incorrect OHS practices, incidents, and nonconformities, organisations may consider creating documented information for that procedure.

The following is a list of potential documented information that organisations may consider necessary for their OHSMS:

Table 7.2   ISO 45001:2018 Potential Documented Information (ISO 45001:2018)

No.	ISO 45001 Clause	Potential Documented Information
1	4.1	List of external and internal issues
2	4.2	List of interested parties and their needs and expectations
3	4.4	OHSMS manual
4	5.3	Organisational structure
5	5.4	Procedure for consultation and participation of workers
6	6.1	Procedure for planning OHSMS
7	6.1.3 & 9.1.2	Procedure for determination and compliance evaluation of legal requirements
8	7.2 & 7.3	Procedure for competence evaluation and training
9	7.4	Procedure for internal and external communication
10	7.5	Procedure for management of documented information
11	8.1	Procedure for operational planning and control
12	8.1.2	Procedure for elimination of hazards and reducing OHS risks
13	8.1.3	Procedure for management of change
14	8.1.4	Procedure for control of procurement of products and services
15	8.2	Procedure for handling of emergency situations
16	9.1	Procedure for monitoring, measurement, analysis, and evaluation of OHS performance
17	9.1.1	Procedure for maintenance and calibration of measuring equipment
18	9.2	Procedure for internal OHSMS audit
19	9.3	Procedure for management review
20	10.2	Procedure for incident investigation
21	10.2	Procedure for nonconformity handling and corrective action

Organisations should have appropriate document control processes to ensure that their documented information can be easily identified when it is being created or updated. Adequate referencing conventions such as title, date, reference number, and author should be used. Documented information should be in an appropriate format (e.g. language, software version, graphics) and medium (e.g. paper, electronic). Documented information should be approved before being disseminated throughout the organisation and regularly reviewed for suitability and adequacy to prevent the circulation of outdated information.

The standard requires organisations to establish a robust document control process to define and implement controls needed to approve, distribute, protect, review, revise, identify changes, retain, dispose of, and provide access to documented information of internal and external origin.

Workers may find it difficult to access certain types of documents if documents are kept a distance from their working area or are password protected. Organisations should ensure that documented information relevant to their OHSMS is suitable to use and easily available to interested parties at the point of use.

Organisations should determine access control and protection of the documented information to prevent unauthorised access and reproduction of confidential information. 'Access' can imply permission to view the documented information only, or the permission to view and change the documented information. Documented information should also be protected from corruption and unintended alteration by physical security (e.g. server rooms, libraries) and IT security (e.g. password, server, backup, encryption, 'read only').

Organisations should determine mechanisms to control changes and updates to documented information such as revision number, date, and disposal of out-of-date and obsolete documents to ensure that older versions have been withdrawn.

Documents that need to be retained for a specific time period should be preserved and stored properly. When considering the retention period for documented information, special consideration should be given to documents with regulatory requirements to ensure that the defined period meets the minimum essential period required.

Documented information control processes should be communicated throughout the organisation to ensure that workers understand what types of information need to be controlled and how this control should be exercised.

Organisations should follow the same mechanism of document control for documents of external origin.

Steps to Complete

1. Determine procedures for control of documented information including:

   a. authorities and responsibilities of document controllers to create, approve, access, revise, archive, and dispose of documents

b. required documented information to effectively manage OHSMS
c. format (e.g. language, software version, graphics), media (e.g. paper, electronic), identification and description (e.g. a title, date, author, or reference number)
d. document numbering and version numbering conventions
e. methodology of storage, preservation, distribution, access, request for change, retention, and withdrawal and disposition of documents
f. control of documents of external origin

Auditors Will Check That the Organisation

- Maintains and retains documented information as required by the ISO 45001
- Controls its documented information by appropriate means
- Approves critical OHS documents before their distribution
- Has a process for retaining and disposing of their documented information
- Has a process for access, control, and protection of documented information
- Ensures there is appropriate access to the health information of workers
- Identifies and controls documents of external origin

Records

- Procedure for management of documented information (non-mandatory)
- List of document controllers, their authorities, and responsibilities (non-mandatory)
- List of required documented information to manage OHSMS (non-mandatory)
- Document modification/change request form (non-mandatory)
- Document issue/receipt note (non-mandatory)
- Document withdrawal notice (non-mandatory)

Chapter 8

Operation

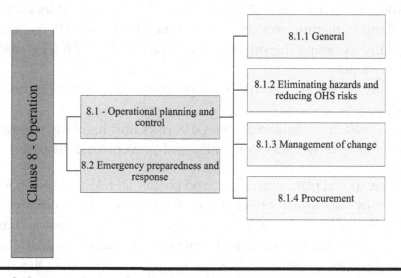

Overview of Clause 8—Operation (ISO 45001:2018).

8.1 Operation Planning and Control

8.1.1 General & 8.1.2 Eliminating Hazards and Reducing OHS Risks

Once processes to meet the requirements of the OHSMS are determined, the standard requires organisations to plan for implementation and control of the processes. Whether it is eliminating hazards, managing risks, or complying with legal health and safety requirements, organisations need to apply some levels of control. Organisations are responsible for taking every

DOI: 10.4324/9781003266532-8

precautionary action reasonably practicable, especially the ones outlined in legislation, to prevent injuries and ill health at their workplace. At multi-employer workplaces, relevant parts of the OHSMS should be coordinated with other organisations.

Typical processes that need to be controlled include consultation and participation of workers, hazard and risk assessments, emergency preparedness and response, internal audits, management reviews, nonconformity, and incident investigations. Organisations should consider best practices and technological advancements when deciding on process controls. Examples of actions that organisations should take to control their OHS-related processes include:

- Reviewing processes and established criteria to monitor their performance to ensure that they cover all the legal and other requirements
- Defining criteria to control the performance of contractors and suppliers
- Regularly evaluating workers' competency for their OHS responsibilities
- Regularly assessing the organisation's compliance with legal and other requirements
- Regularly reviewing internal audit processes and assessing their effectiveness
- Taking proactive steps to assess OHS risks and regularly reviewing the participation of workers to identify and prevent OHS hazards

Organisations should plan, implement, and control all relevant operational areas and activities by establishing operating criteria and control processes while considering 'hierarchy of control' measures for elimination of hazards and reduction of OHS risks. The hierarchy of control provides a structured approach by prioritising control actions to eliminate hazards and reduce or control OHS risks.

The following points demonstrate the sequence of applying a hierarchy of controls shown in Figure 8.1. Each control is considered less effective than the previous one:

1. *Elimination*: removing the hazard (e.g. eliminating a hazardous substance from the process)
2. *Substitution*: replacing the hazard with a less hazardous alternative (e.g. using a safer machine)
3. *Engineering controls/work reorganisation*: isolating people from the hazard (e.g. install extra guarding for a machine)
4. *Administrative controls including training*: changing the way people work (e.g. conduct new operator training)
5. *Personal protective equipment (PPE)*: protecting workers by providing adequate PPE (e.g. utilising safety shoes and glasses)

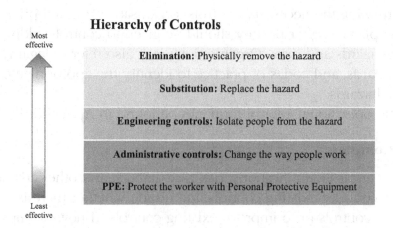

Figure 8.1   Health and safety hierarchy of controls (ISO 45001:2018).

Other factors that organisations should take into account when applying the hierarchy of controls include:

■ Recognising the need for a combination of engineering and administrative controls
■ Establishing good practices in the control of the particular hazard under consideration
■ Adapting work to the individual (e.g. to take account of individual mental and physical capabilities)
■ Taking advantage of technical progress to improve controls
■ Using measures that protect everyone (e.g. by selecting engineering controls that protect everyone in the vicinity of a hazard in preference to giving PPE to the machine operators only)
■ Being aware of human behaviour and whether a particular control measure is acceptable and implementable
■ Identifying typical basic types of human failure (e.g. lapses of memory or attention, lack of understanding or error of judgement, and breach of rules or procedures) and ways of preventing them
■ Introducing planned maintenance of equipment (e.g. machinery safeguards)
■ Recognising the possible need for emergency/contingency arrangements where risk controls fail
■ Acknowledging the potential lack of familiarity with the workplace and existing controls of those not in the direct employment of the organisation (e.g. visitors and contractor personnel)

After determining the necessary controls, organisations should prioritise their action plans. Higher priority should be given to controls addressing significant hazards and risks. Organisations may also refer to legal requirements, standards, and codes of practice to identify the appropriate controls for specific hazards.

A sample operational control form can be found in Appendix F.

Steps to Complete

1. Review hazard identifications, risk assessments, and other critical processes; consider existing controls and decide whether there is a need for new controls or to improve existing controls. If new or improved controls are required, they should be determined by considering the hierarchy of controls (e.g. regular inspection of health and safety equipment, use of secured fences and emergency stops for machinery, valid test and tag of electrical tools).
2. Define acceptable operating criteria for significant hazards in the workplace including speed limits, number of incidents, noise limits, and quantity and type of fire extinguishers required.
3. Regularly review compliance with legal and other requirements.

Auditors Will Check That

■ Critical processes of the organisation have been identified.
■ Adequate control measures have been determined for critical processes.
■ Adequate training on how to apply the hierarchy of controls has been given to workers who determine the control measures.
■ Hierarchy sequence has been considered when determining control measures.

Records

■ Procedures for operational planning and control (non-mandatory):

   * methodology to identify critical processes, control measures, and acceptable criteria
   * authorities and responsibilities of relevant workers
   * process to implement controls in accordance with the criteria
   * process for maintaining and retaining documented information to the extent necessary to have confidence that the processes have been carried out as planned

- List of operational controls (non-mandatory)

  * critical operations
  * significant hazards
  * method of control
  * acceptable operating criteria

- Records of the hierarchy of control training for relevant workers (non-mandatory)

8.1.3 Management of Change

To keep pace with the evolving business environment, organisations are likely to make changes in their structure, processes, products, people, and culture. Changes that can have a noticeable impact on the organisation's OHSMS may include:

- New products, services, and processes, or changes to existing products, services, and processes, including:

  * workplace locations and surroundings
  * work organisation
  * working conditions
  * equipment
  * workforce personnel

- Changes to legal requirements and other requirements
- Changes in knowledge or information about hazards and OHS risks
- Developments in knowledge and technology

Changes can bring risks and these risks should be managed properly to ensure the efficiency of the OHSMS. The standard requires organisations to establish a process to effectively control and manage planned temporary and permanent changes that have an influence on their OHS performance. Organisations should ensure that the new hazards and risks are all identified and control measures are evaluated before changes are implemented. Organisations should utilise suitable methods to manage changes, depending on the nature of the change. When determining processes to manage temporary and permanent changes, organisations should:

1. Identify potential hazards, risks and opportunities associated with the change.

2. Evaluate existing and required control measures.
3. Communicate the change, potential hazards, risks, opportunities, and control measures to all relevant parties.
4. Implement the change and control measures.
5. Regularly monitor and review the change.

In the case of unintended changes (e.g. Covid-19 pandemic), organisations should review the consequences and take necessary actions to mitigate any adverse effects.

Resistance to change from workers is a natural barrier in every organisation because humans have an inherent resistance to moving out of their comfort zone. The level at which the workers feel involved in the development of the change and understand their responsibilities in the change-management process will have a significant impact on the implementation of the change. Top management should regularly reinforce the benefits of the change to workers to ensure they maintain focus and motivation for proceeding with the change.

Steps to Complete

1. Determine a process for change management by:

   a. considering the authorities and responsibilities for implementation, review, and approval of the change
   b. determining how to identify temporary and permanent changes that impact OHS performance, potential hazards and risks and control measures, and how to change the implementation plan

Auditors Will Check That

■ Processes for change management have been determined.
■ The organisation has managed previous changes effectively.
■ Risk assessment was completed before implementation of recent changes.
■ Workers responsible for the implementation of change are competent.

Records

■ List of recent changes in the organisation (non-mandatory), including:

* nature of the change
* justification for the change
* impact on OHS performance and other processes
* resultant benefits

* potential risks and hazards
* required control measures
* responsible workers
* plans to implement the change
* target date
* actual actions taken
* completion date
* review of the effectiveness of the change

8.1.4 Procurement

8.1.4.1 General

The health and safety–related failure of products and equipment is one of the factors that can influence the OHS performance of an organisation. Adequate measures should be taken by organisations to ensure that products, services, equipment, and raw materials with harmful health and safety potential have not been used in their workplace. This can include a hazardous substance in a cleaning solvent or a lack of adequate fences and guards on a machine.

This clause of the standard is about the procurement of goods and services. Organisations should establish a process within their procurement system to ensure that supplied goods and services comply with the requirements of their OHSMS. An organisation's procurement system should have processes for evaluating, selecting, and reviewing external suppliers against the organisation's expectations relevant to health and safety in the workplace. An effective procurement process should include controls that:

■ Identify and assess potential hazards, risks, and opportunities associated with goods and services.
■ Evaluate requirements for goods and services to ensure conformance to OHS objectives.
■ Communicate potential hazards and risks of the goods and services to relevant workers.
■ Evaluate delivered goods and services to ensure they function as intended before being released to workers.

Steps to Complete

1. Define the health and safety specification of products and services needed to be procured.

2. Determine criteria for the selection of the product or service.
3. Determine methodology for assessing and selecting the suppliers.
4. Determine methodology for inspecting and testing incoming materials.
5. Specify the health and safety specifications of products and services to the suppliers.

Auditors Will Check That

■ A process for procurement has been established.
■ Health and safety specifications of incoming products and services are defined.
■ A responsible person(s) understands and is able to explain the methodology for OHS inspection and testing of inward goods and services.
■ The organisation has established a process to inform suppliers about the OHS requirements of the supplied goods and services (e.g. products OHS specifications on the purchase order).

Records

■ Approved suppliers register (non-mandatory)
■ Purchase orders with OHS specifications of products or services (non-mandatory)

8.1.4.2 Contractors

Contractors can offer organisations specialised skills to upscale rapidly while reducing the number of their employees. Organisations use contractors for different types of services such as plumbing, demolition, cleaning, inspection, and maintenance. Contractors working together with the organisation have overlapping health and safety duties. The organisation and its contractors should consult, cooperate, and coordinate their activities to comply with all the OHS requirements of the organisation.

The standard requires organisations to establish a process to manage and control their activities with their contractors to reduce OHS risks and potential hazards. While working for the organisation, either on the organisation's premises or off-site, performing hazardous tasks such as welding, working at height, working with hydraulic machines, or in confined spaces, contractors should comply with the OHS requirements determined by the organisation.

Some of the contractors may not have a comprehensive OHSMS, but organisations should ensure that they do not compromise the health and safety of the organisation or others in the workplace. Organisations should establish an effective process to determine:

- The organisation's activities and operations that impact on the contractors
- The contractor's activities and operations that impact on the organisation
- The contractor's activities and operations that impact on others in the workplace

The contractor management process should provide a scheme for sharing health and safety data to report potential hazards and risks in the workplace to the contractors and receive the contractor's input on hazards and risks that may alert the organisation to a potential OHS risk. This can be achieved through inductions, meetings, risk assessments, accident reports, and so on. It is also the organisation's responsibility to ensure that their contractors comply with OHS regulatory requirements when conducting activities for the organisation.

An effective contractor management process starts with defining contractor selection criteria relevant to the health and safety in the workplace before selecting contractors. These criteria should ensure that the contractor has the capacity to conduct activities in a safe and healthy manner and can comply with the OHSMS and regulatory requirements. Contractors should also be assessed to ensure that they are capable of identifying and reporting potential hazards and are willing to be regularly monitored and reviewed by the organisation.

After selecting an appropriate contractor, the organisation should conduct an initial risks' assessment to identify potential hazards, risks and opportunities associated with the activities of the contractor. Organisations should also define control measures including required PPE and permissions to work, actions required in case of emergencies, training required, and frequency of inspecting and monitoring the contractor's activities.

Before the work begins, a pre-start meeting is a good way to communicate all the OHS information necessary to the contractor and the organisation's OHS policies, objectives, and its expectations of the contractor. The contractor's risk assessments should also be regularly reviewed to ensure that they are in line with the organisation's own identified hazards, risks, and opportunities. It is also the organisation's responsibility to ensure that the contractor's workers are competent to carry out the tasks.

A contractor's OHS performance should be regularly monitored and evaluated to ensure compliance with the agreed requirements. Results of these evaluations should be communicated to the contractors, and any nonconformity should be identified and rectified.

Steps to Complete

1. Conduct a risk assessment to identify potential risks, hazards, and legal requirements associated with the tasks being contracted.
2. Determine a procedure for evaluation and selection of contractors by considering whether contractors:

   a. can perform tasks in a safe and healthy manner
   b. comply with legal OHS requirements
   c. comply with the organisation's OHSMS requirements
   d. are capable of identifying and reporting potential hazards and incidents
   e. have competent workers, the correct equipment, and work permits
   f. are willing to be regularly monitored and reviewed by the organisation

3. Specify the organisation's OHS requirements in the contract.
4. Communicate potential health and safety hazards and risks in the workplace to the contractors and review their hazard and risk assessment in inductions or meetings.
5. Assign responsible person(s) to oversee the contract and regularly monitor the contractor's OHS performance.

Auditors Will Check That

■ The organisation has established a process to determine the risks and hazards of tasks before contracting them out.
■ The organisation has a pre-qualification process and has determined the OHS criteria to be evaluated.
■ OHS requirements have been specified in the contracts.
■ The organisation communicates potential risks and hazards in the working area to the contractors.
■ The organisation ensures that the contractors are informed about any changes in hazard and risk registers.
■ Contractors communicate their OHS risks and hazards with the organisation.
■ The organisation has procedures to manage situations such as multiple contractors on site with overlapping OHS duties.

Records

- Prequalified contractors register (non-mandatory)
- List of potential hazards and risks, probability, and control measures of a task before being contracted (non-mandatory)
- Evidence of contractor evaluation in regard to OHS before awarding the contract (non-mandatory)
- OHS requirements of the organisation specified in the contractual agreement with the contractors (non-mandatory)
- Evidence of communication of risks and hazards between the organisation and contractors (non-mandatory)

8.1.4.3 Outsourcing

Outsourcing refers to a strategy whereby an organisation shifts a part of or the whole task, operation, or process to an external workforce. The difference between outsourcing and purchasing is that in outsourcing the process is being managed by the external contractor on behalf of the requesting organisation while purchasing is supplying a product or service as per specifications previously defined.

Organisations often use an outsourcing strategy when they want to reduce lead times, costs, save resources, mitigate risks, or when they do not have the expertise or capacity to undertake the process directly. Examples of outsourcing activities can include fabrication, assembly, machining, design, project management, inspection, recruitment, etc. The standard requires organisations to take responsibility for compliance with their OHSMS, regulatory and other requirements for the products and services that are being outsourced.

When engaging in outsourcing, organisations should establish a process for the selection of capable providers and evaluation of their performance to comply with the OHSMS and regulatory requirements. Organisations should also determine risks involved in outsourcing and have the means to react to potential problems caused by the external provider that may affect their OHSMS. Organisations should control outsourced products or services by:

- Determining control methodologies required to comply with legal and other requirements
- Communicating legal and other requirements to the provider
- Ensuring OHS controls are being implemented by the provider
- Ensuring that the supplied products and services are consistent with the intended outcomes of the OHSMS

Steps to Complete

1. Conduct a risk assessment to identify potential risks, hazards, and legal requirements associated with the tasks being outsourced.
2. Define control measures for identified risks, hazards, and legal requirements.
3. Determine a procedure for evaluation and selection of providers by considering whether providers:

   a. comply with legal OHS requirements
   b. comply with the organisation's OHSMS requirements
   c. have adequate control measures
   d. are willing to be regularly monitored and reviewed by the organisation

4. Specify the organisation's OHS requirements in the contract.
5. Communicate potential health and safety hazards and risks.
6. Assign responsible person(s) to oversee the contract and regularly monitor the provider's OHS performance.

Auditors Will Check

- That the organisation has determined potential risks, hazards, and legal requirements associated with the tasks being outsourced
- The type and degree of control that is being applied to the outsourced functions
- The criteria that are considered in the selection of the providers
- That the organisation has a process to communicate its legal and other requirements to its providers
- That the provider's OHS performance is reviewed regularly by the organisation

Records

- Approved providers register (non-mandatory)
- List of potential risks, hazards, legal requirements, and control measures for the tasks being outsourced (non-mandatory)
- Provider's pre-qualification in regard to the OHS requirements of the organisation (non-mandatory)
- Communication of OHS requirements of the organisation with its providers (non-mandatory)
- Regular OHS-related evaluation of providers (non-mandatory)

8.2 Emergency Preparedness and Response

Emergency situations are unexpected events that require an immediate response to minimise adverse effects on the health and safety of relevant interested parties including workers, contractors, visitors, and the community. Emergency situations may originate within the organisation or may be an environmental condition that can affect the organisation's OHSMS. Examples of emergency situations can include work-related accidents, earthquakes, floods, fires, explosions, gas leaks, sabotage, and vandalism.

The standard requires organisations to establish, implement, and maintain processes to identify foreseeable emergencies applicable to their operations and define effective plans to respond to these situations. Organisations should take the following steps to prevent, prepare, and respond to potential emergency situations:

1. Establish plans that outline actions to respond to emergencies including the provision of emergency first aid, medical treatment, evacuation, firefighting.
2. Provide training relevant to planned responses to workers at all levels on their emergency situation responsibilities (i.e. first-aiders, fire wardens).
3. Communicate information on emergency situation response plans to all interested parties including workers, contractors, visitors, emergency response services, government authorities, and the local community, and consider their needs and capabilities in assisting and complying with emergency instructions.
4. Periodically rehearse and exercise the planned response capability (e.g. fire drills, evacuation drills, falling from heights drills).
5. Review the performance results of planned responses, and, as needed, revise established emergency plans and communicate them to all relevant parties.
6. Maintain documented information on emergency planning, communication, training, testing, and reviewing performance.

Emergency response plans include written instructions and information to apply controls and measures that will prevent emergency situations in the early stages, and prepare and respond to emergency situations that could not be prevented. Organisations can take the following steps to develop an effective emergency response plan:

1. Identify potential emergency situations and their impacts on all interested parties. When determining potential emergency situations, it is important to consult with people with extensive knowledge of operations (e.g. OHS advisers, operation supervisors, machine operators) and use reliable sources such as previous accident/incident reports, material safety data sheets, and equipment manuals.
2. Provide clear instructions detailing the actions to be taken during the emergency.
3. Maintain a list of hazardous substances and their locations on the organisation's premises to ensure that emergency response teams have access to this information in the event of an emergency.
4. Assign emergency responsibilities to competent workers.
5. Provide training to relevant interested parties.
6. Provide resources required to control emergency situations (e.g. first aid kits, fire extinguishers).
7. Determine an internal and external communication plan during an emergency situation.
8. Define procedures to test and practice the emergency response plans.
9. Develop processes to review results of previous emergency drills, revise plans when required, and communicate changes to interested parties.

Other factors that need to be considered when developing emergency response plans include:

■ Site location
■ Number of workers
■ Shift patterns
■ Existing emergency response equipment (e.g. first aid kit, fire extinguishers, sprinklers)
■ Number of emergency exit doors and assembly points
■ Position and distance to emergency exit routes, doors, and assembly points
■ Cleared areas for the access of emergency services
■ Guidance offered by emergency services

Steps to Complete

1. Determine emergency response plans:

   a. identify all the potential emergency situations for both safety (e.g. fire) and health (e.g. epidemic of an infectious disease)
   b. define emergency contacts
   c. establish emergency response teams
   d. define preventive and emergency response instructions
   e. define required emergency response equipment
   f. determine frequency of emergency drills and equipment testing

2. Communicate emergency plans to relevant parties including workers, contractors, emergency response services, regulatory bodies, and the local community
3. Provide emergency preparedness training and awareness to workers at all levels
4. Periodically rehearse and test emergency plans
5. Evaluate the effectiveness of emergency plans by analysing results from emergency drills and revising plans where required

Auditors Will Check That

■ The organisation has determined an effective emergency preparedness and response plan for both safety (e.g. fire) and health (e.g. epidemic of an infectious disease).
■ The organisation has procedures to communicate the emergency preparedness and response plan to the relevant interested parties including workers at all levels, contractors, and emergency services.
■ Responsibilities in emergency situations have been assigned to competent workers (first-aiders, fire wardens, emergency coordinators).
■ Correct and adequate emergency response equipment is provided (fire extinguishers, first aid kits, fire hose reels, building warrant of fitness, exit signs, assembly points).
■ The organisation conducts regular emergency drills.
■ The organisation evaluates its emergency performance and identifies OFIs.

Records

■ Emergency response plan (mandatory):

   * emergency contact details (e.g. management, supervisors, safety officers, first-aiders, fire wardens, neighbouring businesses, contractors)

* emergency services contact details (e.g. fire department, police, ambulance, medical centre)
* potential emergencies (e.g. fire, gas leak, first aid, flood, earthquake)
* emergency response team
* prevention instructions
* emergency instructions
* location of assembly points
* location of emergency response equipment (e.g. fire extinguishers, fire hose reels, first aid kits)
* frequency of emergency drills
* frequency of testing emergency equipment

■ Records of emergency drills and OFIs (non-mandatory)
■ Records of emergency equipment maintenance (non-mandatory)
■ Records of training for emergency awareness and response teams (non-mandatory)

Chapter 9

Performance Evaluation

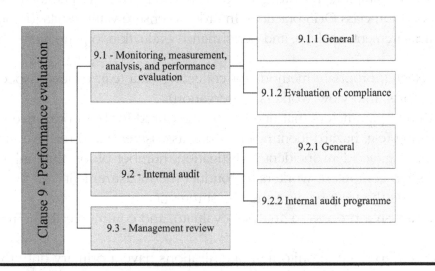

Overview of Clause 9—Performance evaluation (ISO 45001:2018).

9.1 Monitoring, Measurement, Analysis, and Performance Evaluation

To effectively identify opportunities for improvement, organisations should have a systematic approach to the collection of health and safety data from sources available to the organisation, and to assessing their OHS performance. Performance measurement can provide information necessary to improve the OHSMS and assist organisations to determine whether OHS policies and risk control measures have been implemented. Organisations

DOI: 10.4324/9781003266532-9

should evaluate the effectiveness of their OHSMS by collecting data, monitoring, and measuring the following aspects:

■ The extent to which legal and other requirements are fulfilled, and eliminate non-compliance if any
■ The extent to which OHSMS objectives have been achieved, and identify shortcomings
■ Characteristics of operational activities related to identified hazards, risks, and opportunities
■ Effectiveness of operational and other controls

Measuring OHS performance can be done through systematic audits, workplace inspections, sampling, reviewing documents and records, and benchmarking against best-in-class OHS practices. In order to ensure valid results for monitoring, measurement, analysis, and performance evaluation, organisations should:

■ Select appropriate methods for collecting data (e.g. review inspection reports, interview workers, observation)
■ Define parameters that need to be measured for both proactive monitoring (e.g. hazard identification, risk assessment) and reactive monitoring (e.g. accident/incident investigation, number of lost-time injuries)
■ Assign competent workers to conduct the measurement
■ Define the frequency of the measurement
■ Establish a process to analyse, evaluate, and communicate the results

In addition to safety monitoring, organisations have a primary duty to systematically monitor worker health, as far as is reasonably practicable, and detect early signs of ill health or disease of workers exposed to certain health hazards. Health surveillance can help organisations to ensure control measures of health hazards are working effectively. Examples of working conditions that require regular health monitoring include:

■ Workers carry out ongoing work using hazardous substances.
■ Workers carry out asbestos removal work or who are at risk of exposure to asbestos when carrying out the work.
■ Workers exposed to biological hazards such as urine or blood.

An organisation's health monitoring programme should take proactive measures to collect data and detect early signs of ill health and disease. Organisations should ensure that health monitoring is carried out by competent people with adequate knowledge, skills, and experience in health surveillance. Organisations should determine how the health monitoring reports will be evaluated and when to notify authorities or other organisations in the case of overlapping duties.

9.1.1   Maintenance of Monitoring and Measuring Equipment

Organisations use different instruments to measure and monitor their OHS performance. These measuring devices can include temperature gauges, weighing scales, decibel meters, smoke detectors, and voltmeters. To ensure that reliable data is collected, organisations should determine a process for maintenance and calibration of monitoring and measuring equipment. Each item of monitoring and measuring equipment should have a calibration status tag clearly mentioning:

- Equipment identification/asset number
- Date of the last calibration
- Due date of next calibration

Re-calibration checks should be carried out as per schedule and any servicing required should be reported. In case of calibration and servicing done by external providers, calibration certificates and service records obtained from them should be maintained.

   If measuring equipment is found to be out of calibration during its usage, it should be moved to quarantine and any inspection and test conducted using this measuring equipment since the last calibration should be reassessed. Any out-of-calibration equipment is subject to re-calibration before using it again. For monitoring and measuring equipment, the manufacturer's guidelines should be followed for handling, preservation, and storage of equipment.

9.1.2   Evaluation of Compliance

The standard also requires organisations to establish, implement, and maintain a process to regularly evaluate their compliance with legal and other requirements identified in clause 6.1.3 and to define any actions that need to be taken to eliminate non-compliance. Organisations should have a frequent and robust means (evaluations, tests, audits) of ensuring compliance status is maintained. The factors contributing to the failure of compliance with legal and other requirements should be identified, analysed, resolved, and communicated to relevant interested parties.

An effective compliance evaluation programme should determine:

- Evaluation method (compliance assessment audits, consulting with external experts)
- Responsible person(s) to conduct the evaluation
- Frequency of the evaluation depending on past compliance performance and frequency at which legislation is revised
- Gaps and actions required to achieve compliance
- Resources and responsibilities needed to achieve and maintain the compliance
- Current status of compliance obligations (e.g. register of legal obligations)
- Level of integration needed with other evaluation processes such as internal audits

Organisations should retain documented information as evidence of:

- Results of monitoring, measurement, analysis, and performance evaluation
- Maintenance and calibration of measuring equipment
- Results of compliance evaluation

Steps to Complete

1. Establish an OHS monitoring plan:

   a. determine what needs to be monitored (e.g. achievement of an objective, legal obligation, identification of potential hazards in a new process)
   b. define monitoring methods and criteria (e.g. number of incidents occurred, percentage of objectives achieved)
   c. determine the frequency of monitoring (e.g. weekly, quarterly, annually)
   d. determine a calibration system for measuring equipment to ensure results are reliable (e.g. list of OHS measuring devices, frequency of calibration, retaining calibration certificates)
   e. assign responsibility for measurement, monitoring, evaluation, and reporting of results

2. Collect data and analyse OHS performance
3. Define corrective actions
4. Perform corrective actions
5. Review the effectiveness of corrective actions taken
6. Maintain and retain evidence as documented information

Auditors Will Check That

■ A process has been established to determine what needs to be monitored, how, when, and by whom.
■ The organisation has procedures to evaluate its performance results.
■ The organisation has a method to carry out calibration of its measuring equipment.
■ The organisation evaluates conformance to legal and other obligations.
■ The organisation seeks external consultancy to ensure compliance with legal obligations.
■ The organisation keeps up to date regarding its legal obligations.

Records

■ OHS monitoring plan (mandatory) (see Appendix G):

* monitoring factor (e.g. achievement of an OHS objective)
* monitoring methodology (e.g. assess the progress of the objective)
* monitoring criteria (e.g. percentage completed)
* monitoring frequency (e.g. quarterly)
* responsible person to conduct the monitoring and communicate results
* results of monitoring
* corrective action
* verification of corrective action

■ Calibration schedule of monitoring and measuring equipment (mandatory):

* equipment type
* unique identification number
* location of use
* frequency of checking calibration
* method of checking
* responsibility for checking
* acceptance criteria (maximum error)
* actions to be taken for unsatisfactory results

■ Compliance evaluation results (mandatory)

* compliance obligation type (e.g. legal, regulatory, contractual)
* obligation description
* latest version
* consequences of non-compliance

* frequency of review
* responsibility
* current compliance status
* last review date

9.2   Internal Audit

After establishing and implementing an OHSMS, organisations should evaluate and monitor their processes to ensure that their system is delivering its intended outcomes. To assess compliance with the OHSMS and ISO 45001 requirements, organisations should conduct internal audits periodically. Internal audit is a task typically conducted by people within the organisation to provide unbiased and independent reviews of systems and processes. Audits can provide valuable information on the extent that OHS objectives and policies have been achieved and define OFIs. To establish an effective internal audit process, organisations should:

1. Develop an internal audit programme and revise it regularly depending on the previous audits and results of performance monitoring
2. Train and assign competent internal auditors to collect objective evidence concerning the effectiveness of the OHSMS activities
3. Evaluate results of internal audits to identify needs for improvement
4. Define corrective actions for nonconformances and improvements
5. Verify completion of corrective actions and review effectiveness
6. Maintain and retain documentation of execution and analysis of results of internal audits
7. Communicate results of audits to relevant workers

An audit programme is a set of audits planned for a specific time frame and directed towards a specific objective. The complexity of the audit programme depends on factors such as the size and maturity of the organisation. An audit programme should determine:

■ *Frequency*: The standard states that audits should be done at planned intervals but did not establish a specific frequency. Organisations should establish a frequency which is right for their processes. Audits can be done daily, weekly, monthly, quarterly, half-yearly, annually, etc. The frequency of an audit depends on factors such as:

* *complexity of the processes*: critical high-risk operational processes may need to be audited more frequently than low-risk document reviews
* *maturity of the processes*: well-established processes might need auditing once a year while newly developed processes should be audited more frequently
* *previous results*: processes with a history of failures and deficiency should be audited more often

■ *Methodology*: Depending on the intended outcome and organisation activity that is being audited, different internal auditing methods may be utilised. Common methods of internal audits include:

* *System audits*: focusing on the organisation's management system as a whole, this method often uses checklists to ensure that each requirement has been implemented
* *Process audits*: an in-depth evaluation of processes to verify their conformance with the desired outcomes

■ *Responsibilities*: Roles and responsibilities of people involved in internal audits including auditors, auditees, interviewees, and department managers should be clearly defined. These responsibilities may include arrangements for opening and closing meetings, preparation of audit plans, roles of audit team members, and communication of audit findings.

■ *Planning requirements*: When developing an audit programme, organisations should take into consideration factors for effective planning of internal audits. These requirements may include tasks for initiating the audit (e.g. contacting auditees about their availability during the audit, determining the feasibility of the audit) and tasks for preparing audit activities (e.g. preparing the audit plan, preparing checklists and questions).

■ *Consultations*: It is highly important to consult with relevant workers when developing internal audit programmes as this can add valuable information and increase the efficiency of the internal audit results.

■ *Reporting methodology*: Considering objectives, methodology, and scope of the internal audit, organisations should establish and implement an appropriate reporting process to communicate the findings of internal audits. Organisations should define methods to verify the audit results, prepare audit conclusions, conduct exit meetings, and approve and distribute the audit report. The audit report is the final output of the audit and requires appropriate attention. It should contain both positive and negative aspects noted during the audit. Organisations may determine methods of presenting audit reports including an executive summary, observations and key findings, recommendations, OFIs, and graphical representation of findings.

For each audit, organisations should define the criteria against which their conformity will be determined. A well-designed audit usually comprises ISO 45001 requirements, the organisation's OHSMS requirements (e.g. policies, objectives, procedures), and applicable legal and other requirements requested by interested parties. If the organisation is auditing to verify that the requirements of ISO 45001 are implemented, then the requirements of the standard itself become the audit criteria. A sample internal audit report can be found in Appendix H.

Organisations should determine the audit scope for each audit. Audit scope defines the extent and boundaries of an audit, and typically includes a description of physical locations, departments, activities, processes, products, and time period covered.

Conducting effective audits requires specialised knowledge, experience, and skills. Internal auditors should be competent and ideally familiar with the process they are auditing, but they cannot audit their own activities and preferably not their own department. To ensure the OHSMS audit is a reliable tool and provides objective information, organisations should select auditors who follow principles such as:

- *Independence*: being independent of the activity being audited
- *Ethical conduct*: maintaining trust, integrity, and confidentiality
- *Fair presentation*: communicating findings accurately
- *Professional care*: exercising care in accordance with the importance of the task they perform
- *Evidence-based approach*: evidence should be verifiable and based on appropriate sampling
- *Knowledge of the OHSMS internal auditing*: adequate knowledge of ISO 45001, OHSMS, conducting internal audits, and reporting the audit results

The auditor's contribution to the organisation is to provide valuable information for making changes, determining and implementing corrective actions, and continually improving the OHSMS procedures. Audit observations when assessed against audit criteria may result in the following audit findings:

■ *Conformity*: fulfilment of a requirement
■ *Nonconformity*: non-fulfilment of a requirement
■ *Opportunity for improvement*: the requirement has been implemented, but based on the auditor's experience and knowledge, additional effectiveness can be achieved with a modified approach

Auditors should describe the extent to which a requirement has been met. When raising a nonconformance, auditors should clearly define the evidence observed and the requirement that it breaches. A summary of the audit results is typically communicated to the auditees in a closed meeting, followed by a formal written audit report which includes details of observations, the extent to which criteria have been met, and any OFIs.

Audits are a means of helping the organisation, and to be effective, relevant workers should be informed about the OFIs and nonconformities to eliminate the root causes and prevent recurrence. Organisations should establish and implement a process to communicate audit results to relevant personnel including managers, workers, workers' representatives, contractors, and other interested parties where necessary. This is a vital element that is sometimes overlooked.

Organisations should determine the level of information being communicated to the relevant workers. For instance, top management may only need the executive summary of the audit while operational managers and workers may require details of nonconformities and OFIs. It is recommended to include a summary of nonconformances and OFIs as well as compliments (positive observations) in the executive summary of the audit report, as it can provide valuable information for senior management to identify strengths and weaknesses.

Audit results that are communicated to the operational management and workers should clearly explain the nonconformities and OFIs, to assist the team to develop resolution planning (identify root causes and propose corrective actions). When resolution planning has been defined, organisations should allocate required resources including responsible person(s) and define a target date to manage nonconformity. Corrective actions defined should then be implemented within the target dates and their effectiveness should be verified. When an identified nonconformance is not resolved during the audit, follow-up audits shall be conducted.

Organisations should retain documented information as evidence of the implementation of their audit programme and evaluation of results. This evidence may include procedures for internal audits, identified internal audit criteria, annual internal audit schedule, list of competent internal auditors, and internal audit reports.

Steps to Complete

1. Determine a process for the OHSMS internal auditing:

   a. Assign a responsible person for effective implementation of this procedure. Often being allocated to the health and safety manager, the responsible person must identify and train internal auditors, schedule required internal audits, provide resources required, and report the audit results to the senior management.
   b. Define internal audits' required criteria, scope, frequency, methods, responsibilities, resources, target date, consultation, and reporting methods.
   c. Select and train internal auditors on topics such as internal audit processes, responsibilities of internal auditors, requirements of ISO 45001, requirements of the organisation's OHSMS, OHS regulatory requirements, hazard and risk identification, and hierarchy of controls.

2. Conduct internal audits at planned intervals.
3. Define corrective actions for nonconformances and improvements.
4. Report internal audit results to the top management and relevant workers.
5. Conduct follow-up audits and verify completion of corrective actions.
6. Regularly review the effectiveness of internal audit procedures.

Auditors Will Check That

- The organisation has established an internal audit process.
- Appropriate criteria are being evaluated in internal audits.
- The internal auditors are competent.
- The auditors are independent of the activity being audited.
- Internal audits are being conducted at planned intervals.
- The organisation has procedures to communicate audit findings to top management and other relevant managerial and non-managerial workers.

■ Nonconformities identified have been actioned accordingly.
■ The organisation has a system to manage OFIs identified in internal audits.
■ The organisation regularly reviews the effectiveness of its internal audit programme.

Records

■ Internal audit plan (mandatory):

* responsible person(s) for implementation of the plan
* list of internal auditors
* annual audit schedule
* internal audit criteria
* internal audit scope
* audit process
* process for recording and reporting audit results
* verification of effectiveness, closing nonconformities, and OFIs

■ Internal audit report (mandatory):

* audit scope
* audit date
* opening meeting attendees and minutes
* audit criteria and observations
* closing meeting attendees and minutes
* identified nonconformances and OFIs

9.3   Management Review

Overall performance of the OHSMS should be regularly reviewed by top management. The standard does not require a formal meeting to be held as long as senior management is involved in reviewing the information on the performance of the OHSMS. But documented MRMs are good practices to demonstrate management's commitment to health and safety in the workplace.

A management review is an important part of the standard, providing an opportunity for senior management to critically assess the suitability, adequacy, and effectiveness of the established management system. Senior management should ensure that the established OHSMS is:

■ *Suitable*: fits the organisation, its objectives, culture, and operations
■ *Adequate*: implemented as planned
■ *Effective*: achieves its intended outcomes

Inputs from management reviews are documents, data, and performance results, which need to be reviewed by the senior management. Decisions and actions required to rectify the nonconformities and improve the OHS performance of the organisation are the outputs of management reviews. Several input factors need to be regularly reviewed by the top management, including changes in the external and internal issues affecting the OHSMS and identified nonconformities and OFIs. The standard requires organisations to frequently review the following aspects of their health and safety management system:

■ The status of decisions and actions from previous management reviews
■ Changes in:

* the needs and expectations of interested parties (clause 4.2)
* legal requirements and other requirements (clause 6.1.3)
* risks and opportunities (clause 6.1.1)

■ The extent to which the policy and objectives have been met (clauses 5.2 & 6.2.2)
■ The organisation's OHS performance, including trends in:

* incidents, nonconformities, corrective actions, and continuing improvement (clause 10.2)
* monitoring and measurement results (clause 9.1)
* results of evaluation of compliance with legal requirements and other requirements (clause 9.1.2)
* audit results (clause 9.2)
* results of consultation and participation of workers that can lead to identifying OHS concerns and suggestions for improvement (clause 5.4)
* risks and opportunities (clause 6.1.1)

■ The adequacy of resources for maintaining an effective OHSMS (clause 7.1)

■ Relevant communication(s) with internal and external interested parties (clause 7.4.3)
■ Opportunities for continual improvement (clause 10.3)

Organisations do not need to review all of these inputs in every meeting. But they are required to regularly check their performance against these factors. Results of management reviews, including decisions and actions required, should be retained by the organisation as documented information so that they can be appropriately communicated and consulted with relevant interested parties. Management review results should be consistent with the organisation's commitment to continual improvement. Outputs of the management reviews can assist organisations to obtain a clear understanding of issues such as:

■ Is the performance of the established OHSMS at an acceptable level?
■ Is there any opportunity to improve the performance of the OHSMS? If so, what actions are required? Who is responsible? What resources are required? What is the target date?
■ Is there any nonconformity with the legal and other requirements? If so, what actions are required? Who is responsible? What resources are required? What is the target date?
■ Has something happened since the previous management reviews that requires a change in the OHSMS processes or objectives?

It is vital to communicate the outputs of the management reviews to relevant interested parties including workers, workers' representatives, contractors, and other concerned individuals. MRMs should be chaired by a member of top management. Other attendees can be operational management, supervisors, workers' representatives, relevant workers, and, when necessary, internal auditors. It is recommended that the minutes of the meeting be recorded, noted, and later communicated to all attendees.

The standard has not specified a time period for conducting management reviews. But they should be done regularly, consistent with the level of risks and complexity of the organisation. Reports and meeting minutes should be retained as evidence of implementing management reviews.

A sample management review meeting minutes can be found in Appendix I.

Steps to Complete

1. Establish a process for management reviews, including:

   a. responsibilities of senior management and attendees
   b. management review method
   c. frequency
   d. agenda
   e. methodology for communication of results to the concerned individuals

2. Conduct management reviews at planned intervals, specifying:

   a. date and time
   b. attendees
   c. agenda
   d. meeting minutes
   e. actions required

3. Communicate management review decisions and required actions to the concerned individuals

Auditors Will Check That

- The organisation has an established management review process.
- The frequency of the management reviews is established.
- The inputs of management reviews are identified.
- Senior management attends and chairs the management reviews.
- Outputs of management reviews are retained and communicated to relevant individuals.
- The organisation monitors the progress of actions obtained from previous management reviews.

Records

- Procedure for management reviews (non-mandatory)
- Evidence of conducting management reviews (e.g. MRM) (mandatory)

  * date and time
  * attendees
  * agenda
  * meeting minutes
  * actions required

Chapter 10

Improvement

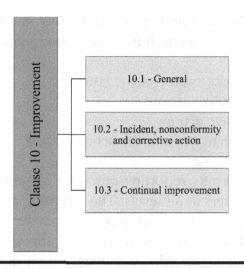

Overview of Clause 10—Improvement (ISO 45001:2018).

10.1 General & 10.2 Incident, Nonconformity, and Corrective Action

Organisations should take proactive approaches to improve their OHSMS. The standard requires organisations to review the results of their OHSMS performance obtained from different sources of OHS data, to identify OFIs and take actions to implement these improvements. Potential sources of the OHS data that can assist with identifying OFIs include management reviews, internal audits, compliance reviews, previous nonconformances and corrective actions.

DOI: 10.4324/9781003266532-10

Organisations should establish a process to systematically identify OFIs, determine plans to achieve them, and action these plans. Improvement of the OHSMS can be done through different OHS functions such as hazards and risks' reduction, training, OHS policy and objectives, and applying control measures.

Potential improvements can also be identified with reactive measures through corrective actions of incidents (e.g. injury, ill health, near misses) and nonconformances (e.g. non-fulfilment of a legal requirement or OHS procedure). Thus, organisations should determine processes to report and investigate incidents and nonconformities, take corrective actions, and properly manage the consequences. These processes should include:

■ Reacting to the incident and/or nonconformity in a timely manner to control, correct, and contain immediate consequences of the incident or nonconformity
■ Investigating the root causes of the issue
■ Determining corrective actions
■ Taking the corrective actions
■ Reviewing the effectiveness of the actions taken

Incident and nonconformity reporting processes should be established and communicated to workers at all levels. The reporting process can be done through incident and nonconformity report forms, sending an email, and verbal reporting to workers' representatives and supervisors. It is necessary to establish effective reporting channels and encourage workers to use them, as many minor injuries, near misses, and nonconformances go unreported.

On the occurrence of an incident, immediate action is required to prevent further injury and to help injured persons. If the OHSMS has been established properly, organisations should have already identified most of the potential hazards, risks, and emergency situations and have procedures in place to manage them. Once the incident is appropriately controlled, organisations should inspect the incident, collect accurate data, conduct interviews, and analyse the sequence of events to identify the root causes and corrective actions required.

'Root cause' refers to the core issue that caused the incident or nonconformity and should be permanently eliminated. Root cause analysis is the practice of detecting the highest-level factors associated with the problem that, when resolved, can prevent a recurrence of the incident or nonconformity.

A typical technique to identify root causes of incidents and nonconformities is the 'five whys' method. It is a simple but powerful approach to reveal the underlying causes. The five whys technique is to simply ask "why?" five times (or enough times) when a problem is encountered until you get past the symptoms of the issue and down to the root causes. This approach is most effective when the answers come from workers who have adequate knowledge and experience of the processes being examined.

Incident investigations should remain impartial and objective to collate clear and accurate information. An example of a hazard/incident/nonconformity report flowchart is demonstrated in Appendix C.

Relevant interested parties including workers, workers' representatives, and contractors should be actively involved in the investigation process of incidents and nonconformities, identification of root causes, and determination of corrective actions. The level of investigation required is associated with the consequences of the incident and its nonconformity. Results of these investigations should be documented and communicated internally and, where appropriate, externally to authorities and regulatory bodies.

When necessary, other organisational units and departments should be informed of the investigation results as it is possible that the same root cause exists in other working areas. OHS risk assessments should be reviewed to verify whether or not the incident and its consequences have been previously identified. If not detected before, it should be added to the risk register to ensure prevention of a reoccurrence and managed using the hierarchy of controls. OHS risks should be assessed for new and changed hazards, prior to taking corrective actions.

If the incident occurred as a result of changes in the OHS procedures, organisations should review their management-of-change process and revise it accordingly to avoid similar issues. Depending on the severity of the incident and root causes identified, it may be necessary to make appropriate changes to the OHSMS.

Documented information should be retained as evidence of investigation of the incident and/or nonconformity, root causes and corrective actions need to be identified, and a review undertaken of the effectiveness of the corrective actions.

A sample incident/accident report form can be found in Appendix J.

A sample nonconformance report form can be found in Appendix K.

Steps to Complete

1. Determine a process for handling incidents and nonconformities, including:

   a. authorities and responsibilities (e.g. persons to communicate incidents and nonconformities to management and authorities; persons to investigate incidents and nonconformities)
   b. methodologies for

      i.   reporting incidents and nonconformities
      ii. investigating incidents and nonconformities
      iii. communicating results and findings to concerned workers
      iv. taking corrective and preventive actions
      v.   verifying the effectiveness of actions taken

2. Consult with workers at all levels while developing procedures for handling incidents and nonconformities
3. Communicate procedures for handling incidents and nonconformities to workers at all levels
4. Select a competent person(s) to communicate incidents and nonconformities to management and authorities
5. Select a competent person(s) to investigate incidents and nonconformities
6. Provide training and encourage workers to report incidents and nonconformities
7. Implement procedures for handling incidents and nonconformities
8. Retain documented information as evidence of incident and nonconformity investigations, corrective actions taken, and the review of their effectiveness

Auditors Will Check

- That the organisation has adequate processes in place to systematically identify OFIs
- What OFIs have been identified
- How the organisation handles these OFIs
- That the organisation has established a process for handling incidents and nonconformities
- How the organisation selects competent persons to investigate incidents and nonconformities
- That workers are aware of how to report incidents and nonconformities

- That workers report minor incidents including near misses
- How the organisation investigates incidents and nonconformities and determines root causes
- How the organisation proposes and takes corrective and preventive actions
- That the organisation reviews effectiveness of actions taken
- That incident and nonconformity reports are communicated to top management
- How the organisation consults with workers in incident prevention
- How the organisation looks for trends in incidents and nonconformities to identify OFIs

Records

- Procedure for handling incidents and nonconformities (non-mandatory)
- Incident investigation report (mandatory)
- Nonconformity investigation report (mandatory)

10.3   Continual Improvement

Most successful organisations in terms of health and safety in the workplace are the ones that are never satisfied with the status quo. They understand the importance of continual improvement and constantly have their eyes on the next level of OHS performance. Thus, the final clause of the standard is to ensure that the organisation's OHSMS is progressively improving and maturing.

Continual improvement is a systematic approach to detecting and implementing OFIs that can help the organisation to accelerate its performance. Continual improvement is embodied in many clauses of the ISO 45001 standard, from regularly reviewing the context of the organisation to finding corrective actions for the nonconformances. This clause is more about establishing a culture that will lead organisations to always determine how they can perform better in regard to OHS.

The standard introduces five requirements to demonstrate the continual improvement of an OHSMS:

- Enhancing OHS performance by considering factors to strengthen health and safety performance including minimising OHS hazards and risks and meeting OHS policy and objectives

- Promoting a culture that provides support to the OHSMS by advocating the commitment of all workers, especially senior management, in supporting the OHS processes
- Promoting the participation of workers in the identification and implementation of actions for continual improvement of the OHSMS—non-managerial workers can provide invaluable information to improve OHSMS, and ISO 45001 highly emphasises their contribution to identifying and actioning the potential improvements
- Communicating the relevant results of continual improvement to workers, and workers' representatives to improve their OHS performance and motivations
- Maintaining and retaining documented information as evidence of continual improvement, which can be extracted from various sources including management reviews, internal audits, OHS objectives, etc.

Organisations should bear in mind that even if their OHS performance is going really well, there are always OFIs. Examples of events and circumstances that can offer potential improvement opportunities include:

- Suggestions and recommendations from interested parties that can provide valuable information on the OHS performance of the organisation and how it can be improved (e.g. staff suggestion box, customer/contractor/supplier feedback scheme, focus groups)
- Sharing lessons learned from incidents and near misses with other organisations
- New technology that can provide better health and safety processes (e.g. less noise, safer equipment, replacement of a hazardous substance in a process)
- New or improved materials that reduce OHS risks to individuals
- Changes in workers competency through training and updating their knowledge and skills

Steps to Complete

1. Determine a process to receive and review feedback and suggestions from workers, contractors, customers, and other interested parties
2. Benchmark best practices used by other organisations in the industry and share lessons learned with other organisations
3. Identify top OHS hazards and risks in the workplace and seek new technologies and materials to reduce the risks

4. Provide OHS training to workers at all levels
5. Review OHSMS processes to ensure opportunities for continual improvement have been identified and actioned

Auditors Will Check

■ How workers were involved in detecting and implementing OFIs
■ How the organisation promotes a culture of continual improvement, and if top management is involved in promoting this culture
■ What actions have been taken to identify and implement opportunities for continual improvement
■ How the results of continual improvement processes are communicated to relevant parties
■ What documented information is available as evidence of continual improvement

Records

■ Workers, contractors, and clients' suggestion and feedback programme (non-mandatory) (A sample OHS suggestion programme and OHS suggestion form can be found in Appendices L and M, respectively.):

* objectives of the programme
* method to submit suggestions and feedback
* responsibilities of person(s) receiving the suggestions and feedback
* responsibilities of person(s) approving the suggestions and feedback
* methodology to review the suggestions and feedback
* process to report the results to the individuals initiating the suggestions and feedback
* suggestion and feedback form

■ Evidence of identifying and implementing OFIs through (mandatory):

* conducting management reviews
* conducting internal audits
* benchmarking best practices in the industry
* providing OHS training to managerial and non-managerial workers
* obtaining new technologies and materials to reduce OHS risks and hazards

Appendices

Appendix A

A Sample Occupational Health and Safety Policy Statement (Clause 5.2)

Company X recognises its moral and legal responsibility to provide a safe and healthy work environment for workers (including contractors and workers of contractors), clients and visitors to the workplace. Our aim is to encourage a positive health and safety culture within the workplace. To ensure this occurs, health and safety will be actively promoted throughout the organisation by the provision of information, training, instruction, and supervision. Company X will openly encourage all staff and contractors to report hazards, including near misses, without fear of reprisal.

Our OHS policy is to strive for a safer and healthier workplace by virtue of:

- Prevention of injury and ill health
- Reducing OHS risks and eliminating hazards
- Establishing effective health and safety objectives, in consultation with our workers and other interested parties
- Train, educate, and inform our workers about OHS issues that may affect their work
- Promote OHS awareness within the company and encourage workers to participate in the decision-making processes within the OHSMS
- Continual improvement in OHSMS

- Continual improvement in OHS performance, and
- Compliance with all applicable legal and other requirements.

Our health and safety policy is reviewed annually and is freely available to all of our interested parties.

Signature: Date:

Appendix B

A Sample Health and Safety Roles, Responsibilities, and Authorities (Clause 5.3)

Responsibility Matrix	Role			
Activity	Top Management	H&S Manager	Head of Department	Worker
Approve OHS policy and objectives	R	A	C/I	C/I
Define a procedure for internal OHS audit	A	R	C/I	C/I
Report concerns, injuries, and near misses	I	C	I	R
Arrange for emergency drills	C	R	I	I
Raise an OHS nonconformance	R	R	R	I
Approve or change the OHSMS procedure	R	C	C	I
Carry out corrective action(s)	A	R	R	C/I

R—Responsible, A—Accountable, C—Consulted, I—Informed

Responsibilities
Position: Managing Director • Take overall responsibility and accountability for OHS for preventing work-related injuries and ill health and providing safe and healthy workplaces. • Ensure that the OHS policy and OHS objectives are established and implemented • Ensure that the requirements of the OHS system, such as hazard identification, risk assessment, application of controls, monitoring, audits, and employee participation are integrated into all work processes
Position: Health and Safety Manager • Manage and mentor the health and safety officers • Monitor health and safety risks and hazards in the workplace • Managing emergency procedures
Position: Head of Departments • Ensuring OHSMS implementation in their department conforms to the company objectives • Allocating required resources from their department to complete OHSMS tasks • Consult with workers on OHS matters
Position: Worker • Take reasonable care for his or her own health and safety • Take reasonable care that his or her acts or omissions do not adversely affect the health and safety of other persons • Report concerns, injuries, and near misses to HSRs and supervisors

Appendix C

A Sample OHS Issue Resolution Procedure Flowchart (Clauses 5.4 & 10.2)

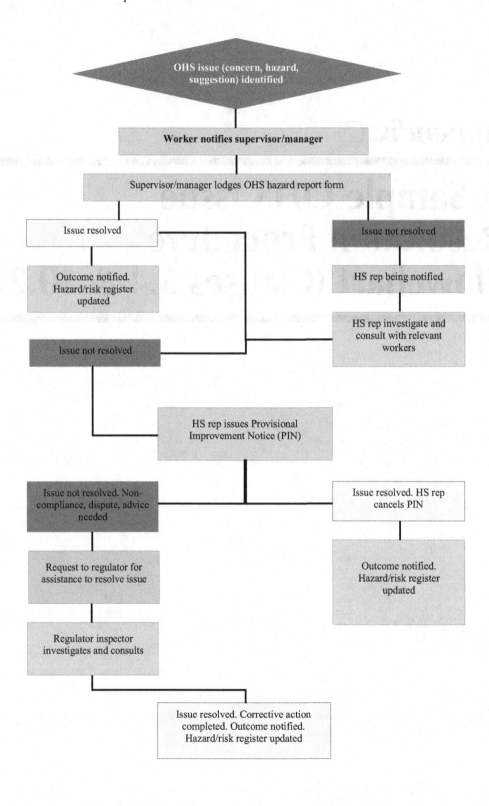

Appendix D

A Sample Permit to Work (PTW) (Clause 7.2)

Permit to Work

To be returned to the responsible officer on completion of the work.

Permission granted to:	
To carry out:	Cutting/Burning/Welding/......................
To use (equipment):	
Location:	
On date://	From (time) .... to (time) ....
Description of work:	

1. All combustible materials removed or made safe	☐
2. No flammable liquids, vapours, gases, or dust present	☐
3. Barricades, warning signs, spark/flash screens provided	☐
4. Fire extinguishers/hoses provided on site	☐
5. Operator knows how to use fire equipment	☐
6. Operator knows location of telephone/fire alarm	☐
7. Site inspected after completion of work	☐

Permit issued by: **Signature:**

Appendix E

A Sample OHS Related Internal and External Communication Procedure (Clause 7.4)

What to Communicate?	ISO 45001: 2018 Cl. Ref.	When?	With Whom?	How?	Who Communicates?
The importance of effective OHS management and conforming to the OHSMS requirements	5.1.e	During OHSMS planning meeting	HODs	Verbally	MD
OHS policy	5.2	After making/ modifying	To all	In writing (display)	MD
Responsibilities and authorities for relevant roles	5.3	After joining/role change	Employees	In writing	MD, Head (P&A)
Hazard identification and assessment of risks and opportunities	6.1.2	After conducting assessments	To the MD and all HODs	In writing	HMR
OHS objectives	6.2.1	During OHSMS planning meeting	HODs	Verbally and in writing	MD
OHS requirements relevant to the organisation (for services and materials to be provided at our site/ our customer's site by the external providers)	8.1.4	Prior to purchase	External providers, including contractors	Verbal and/or in writing	Head (Purchase & Stores)
Relevant OHS performance information	9.1	After evaluation	Internally (to all HODs) and externally (to relevant interested parties)	In writing	HMR

Description	Clause	When	Interested parties who send the communication	Communication method	Responsible
Relevant communication received from interested parties, including complaints	9.3	After reviewing the communication		In writing	MD or HMR
Reporting the results of OHSMS audits to relevant management	9.2.2	After each audit	MD	In writing	HMR
Reporting on the performance of the OHSMS, including OHS performance, to top management	9.3	During management review meeting	MD	In writing	HMR, HODs
Replying to tender documents and purchase orders specifying customers' OHSMS requirements, ISO 45001 certification requirements, etc.	NA	Pre-sales negotiations	Prospective customers	In writing	Head (Marketing)
Information regarding areas of OHSMS hazards within our premises	NA	After identifying OHSMS hazards	Employees, visitors	Display boards	HMR/Head (P&A)
Enquiring about emergency service and contact details	8.2	When such need is felt	Emergency Service Providers	Verbally/In writing	HMR

What to Communicate?	ISO 45001: 2018 Cl. Ref.	When?	With Whom?	How?	Who Communicates?
Enquiring about insurance proposals regarding potential emergencies	8.2	When such need is felt	Insurers	Verbally/In writing	HMR
Responding to audit findings, show-cause notices, intimations, OHSMS requirements, etc.	7.4	After receiving such communications	Government or regulatory body inspectors	In writing	HMR
Responding to letters, certification service offers, audit schedules, audit findings, etc.	7.4	After receiving such communications	ISO 45001 certification body	Verbally/In writing	HMR

Appendix F

A Sample Operational Control Form (Clauses 8.1.1 & 8.1.2)

Operation	Significant Hazard(s)	Method of Control	Acceptable Operating Criteria
Factory/office			
Equipment installation/ dismantling projects			
Marketing & advertising			
Administrative offices			
Purchasing			
Job contracting			
Raw material handling and storage			
Production and maintenance			
R&D, design, engineering			
Laboratory			
Product storage			
Packing and dispatch			
Transportation			
On-site product installation/ maintenance			

Appendix G

A Sample OHS Monitoring Plan (Clause 9.1)

Factor	Method	Criteria	Frequency	Owner	Monitoring Result	Corrective Action	Verification
Requirements from interested parties including legal requirements	Assess list of interested parties and their requirements	Percentage completed	Annually				☐
Identification of hazards, risks, and opportunities	Assess risk register and actions taken	Percentage completed	Half-yearly				☐
Achievement of WHS objectives	Assess organisation's WHS objectives	Percentage completed	Quarterly				☐
Effectiveness of WHS controls	Assess internal audit results	Number of assessed internal audits	Annually				☐
Reduction of incidents	Assess previous accidents and incidents	Number of incidents	Annually				☐

A Sample OHS Monitoring Plan (Clause 9.1)

Appendix H

A Sample Internal Audit Report (Clause 9.2)

Internal Audit Report	
Serial No.	
Internal audit name	
Lead auditor	
Additional auditors	
Auditee(s)	
Checklist name	
Scheduled date	
Department	
Process	
Location	
Audit Findings/Summary:	
Opening Meeting	
Date, time, and duration	
Attendee(s)	
Meeting minutes	
Closing Meeting	
Date, time, and duration	
Attendee(s)	
Meeting minutes	

Internal Audit Questions			
Clause Number	Audit Question	Audit Finding (Compliant, Non-compliant, Opportunity for Improvement)	Observation
6.1.2.1	Does the organisation establish, implement, and maintain a process for hazard identification that is ongoing and proactive?		
6.1.2.1	Does the organisation's processes for hazard identification take into account how work is organised, social factors (including workload, work hours, victimisation, harassment, and bullying), leadership, and the culture in the organisation?		
6.1.2.1	Does the organisation's processes for hazard identification take into account routine and non-routine activities and situations, including hazards arising from infrastructure, equipment, materials, substances, and the physical conditions of the workplace?		
6.1.2.1	Does the organisation's processes for hazard identification take into account routine and non-routine activities and situations, including product and service design, research, development, testing, production, assembly, construction, service delivery, maintenance, and disposal?		
6.1.2.1	Does the organisation's processes for hazard identification take into account routine and non-routine activities and situations, including human factors?		

A Sample Management Review Meeting Minutes (Clause 9.3)

Management Review Meeting (MRM)		
Serial number		
Date and time		
Attendees		
MRM Agenda	Document and Data Reviewed	Minutes
Review of follow-up actions from last OHS MRM	Action plan document of last meeting	
Review of changes that can affect OHSMS	Any recent internal and external changes	
Review of changes in OHS legislation/statutory requirements, legal compliance, needs and expectations of interested parties	Legal and other requirement register, needs and expectations of interested parties	
Review of changes in risk and opportunity register	Risk and opportunity register	
Extent to which the policy and objectives have been met	Updated OHS policy, progress of OHS objectives	
Status of incidents, nonconformities, corrective actions, and continual improvement	Incident reports, nonconformance reports, corrective and preventive action reports	

Monitoring and measurement results	OHS monitoring plan, results of OHS monitoring	
Results of evaluation of compliance with legal requirements and other requirements	Annual compliance evaluation register	
Review of results of internal audits	Latest internal audit reports	
Review of the results of workers' participation and consultation	Toolbox meeting minutes, OHS committee meeting minutes, worker's suggestions, concerns, and complaints	
Adequacy of resources required for maintaining an effective OHSMS	Reports from different departments regarding resources required	
Review of communications with interested parties	Latest communication with internal and external parties especially with regulatory bodies	
Review of recommendations for improvement, opportunities for continual improvement	Recommendations received from managerial and non-managerial workers, contractors, visitors, customers, and other interested parties	
MRM Action Plan		
Task	*Responsibility*	*Target Date*

Appendix J

A Sample Incident/Accident Report Form (Clause 10.2)

Incident Report	
Date	
Department	
Location	
Reported by	
Injured/involved person details	
Name	
Date of birth	
Contact number	
Hours worked before the incident	
Injury type	
Incident details:	
Accident/incident criticality	☐Low ☐Medium ☐High
Type of treatment given	
Name of first-aider involved	
Emergency services or authorities advised?	☐Yes ☐No

Root Cause Analysis	
Why did this incident occur?	
Because	
Ok, but why?	
And why was that?	
Now, what is the overall root cause?	
Date	
Completed by	

Preventive Action		
Proposed Preventive Action	*Responsibility*	*Target Date*
Completed by:	Date:	

Actual Actions Taken	
Actual corrective actions taken:	
Date	
Completed by	

Review of Effectiveness	
Corrective action verified	☐Yes ☐No
Reviewer notes:	
Date	
Completed by	

Appendix K

A Sample Nonconformance Report Form (Clause 10.2)

Nonconformance Report	
Date	
Department	
Location	
Reported by	
Nonconformance details:	
Primary responsibility	
Secondary responsibility	
Nonconformance criticality	☐Low ☐Medium ☐High
Root Cause Analysis	
Why did this incident occur?	
Because	
Ok, but why?	
And why was that?	
Now, what is the overall root cause?	
Date	
Completed by	

Corrective Action		
Proposed Corrective Action	*Responsibility*	*Target Date*
Completed by:	Date:	

Actual Actions Taken
Actual corrective actions taken:

Date	
Completed by	

Review of Effectiveness	
Corrective action verified	☐Yes ☐No
Reviewer notes:	

Date	
Completed by	

Appendix L

A Sample OHS Suggestion Programme (Clause 10.3)

Worker's Suggestion Programme

At company X, we are determined to continuously develop our OHS processes, refine our procedures, and ultimately improve the health and safety of our workers. Company X recognises the power of workers' participation in continual improvement. Workers are in an excellent position to see where opportunities to improve health and safety and working conditions exist. Workers are the best resource for suggesting ways to do things better. With such help, company X can improve its OHS performance.

The primary objective of this programme is to generate productive suggestions for improving health and safety at the workplace. The worker's suggestion programme provides an avenue whereby workers can freely submit their ideas for consideration.

All workers may submit their suggestions to their managers/supervisors by completing the worker's suggestion form. Managers/supervisors are responsible to review the suggestion and approve if it is an eligible suggestion and inform other managers in the next MRM. An eligible suggestion is a positive and complete written suggestion on how we can improve our current OHSMS and procedures. An eligible suggestion should identify a specific problem or deficiency along with a solution. If the implementation of the suggestion is to be initiated, the employee will be advised.

Senior manager signature:

Date:

Appendix M

A Sample OHS Suggestion Form (Clause 10.3)

Worker's Suggestion Form			
Employee Name:		**Date:**	
Department:	☐ Workshop ☐ Production ☐ Design ☐ Finance ☐ Administration ☐ Sales		
How to make your suggestion: • Each suggestion should state a specific health and safety issue, define its cause, and propose definite solutions. • Submit your suggestion by giving it to your manager/supervisor.			
Suggestion Topic:			
Description of Health and Safety Issue:			
Description of Proposed Solution:			
Detail of Benefits:			
Approver's Signature: **Date:**			

References

1. ISO/TC 283. (2018). ISO 45001:2018—Occupational health and safety management systems—Requirements with guidance for use. ISO.
2. Jordan, T. (2019). The ISO 45001: 2018 implementation handbook: Guidance on building an occupational health and safety management system. *Quality Progress*, 52(1), 54–54.
3. Sadiq, N. (2019). Establishing an occupational health & safety management system based on ISO 45001. IT Governance Ltd.
4. HaSPA (Health and Safety Professionals Alliance). (2012). The core body of knowledge for generalist OHS professionals. Tullamarine, VIC. Safety Institute of Australia.
5. ISO/TMBG. (2018). ISO 19011:2018—Guidelines for auditing management systems. ISO.Productivity Press.

Index

Note: Page numbers in *italics* indicate a figure and page numbers in **bold** indicate a table on the corresponding page.

A

action, 58–61; *see also* corrective action
administrative controls, 84
analysis, 99–104
audit, 11
  findings, 11
  four-step audit programme, *9*
  internal, 104–109, 139–140
auditors
  context of the organisation, 18
  improvement, 116–117, 119
  leadership, 21, 23, 24, 25, 27, 28, 29,
    31, 35
  operation, 86, 88, 90, 92, 94, 97
  performance evaluation, 103, 108–109, 112
  planning, 48, 53, 55, 57, 61, 63–64
  support, 66, 69, 72, 75, 81
authorities, 125–126
avoidance, 51
awareness, 70–73

B

biological hazard, 40
biomechanical hazard, 40

C

certification, 7–10
change
  management of, 87–89

chemical hazard, 40–41
clauses, 6–7, **6**
  context of the organisation, 6, 13–18, *13*
  improvement, 7, 113–119, *113*
  leadership and worker participation, 6,
    19–35, *19*
  operation, 7, 83–98, *83*
  performance evaluation, 7, 99–112, *99*
  planning, 6, 37–64, *37*
  support, 7, 65–81, *65*
commitment, 20–28
communication, 73–76, 131–134
competence, 11, 67–70
compliance
  evaluation of, 101–104
conformity, 11, 107
consultation, 11, 105
  of workers, 31–35
context of the organisation, 13–18
continual improvement, 11, 117–119;
    see also improvement
contractors, 90–93
control
  of hazard, 51–53
  hierarchy of, *85*
  of operation, 83–95
corrective action, 11, 113–117

D

definitions, *see* terms and definitions
documented information, 11, 76–81, **77–79**

153

Printed in the United States
by Baker & Taylor Publisher Services